The Self Imagined

The Self Imagined

Philosophical reflections on
the social character of psyche

Karen Hanson

ROUTLEDGE & KEGAN PAUL
New York and London

To my mother
and
in memory of my father

*First published in 1986
by Routledge & Kegan Paul plc*

*Published in the USA by
Routledge & Kegan Paul Inc.
in association with Methuen Inc.
29 West 35th Street, New York, NY 10001*

11 New Fetter Lane, London EC4P 4EE

*Set in 10 on 12 point Times
by Fontwise
and printed in Great Britain
by Thetford Press Ltd
Thetford, Norfolk*

Copyright © Karen Hanson 1986

*No part of this book may be reproduced in
any form without permission from the publisher,
except for the quotation of brief passages
in criticism*

Library of Congress Cataloging in Publication Data

*Hanson, Karen, 1948–
The self imagined.
Includes index.
1. Self (Philosophy) 2. Imagination.
3. Mead, George Herbert, 1863–1931. I. Title.
BD450.H274 1986   126   85-28098*

British Library CIP data also available

ISBN 0–7102–0559–7

CONTENTS

Acknowledgments	vii
Introduction	1
Chapter 1: Mead's theory of the self	14
Motivation for and terms of Mead's account	14
Mead's account: Phylogeny	17
Mead's account: Ontogeny	22
Preliminary criticisms	27
Chapter 2: Imagination	42
Mead on imagination	42
Sartre compared with Mead	46
Sartre on imagination	48
Accommodation within another view	57
Seeing . . . as . . . and contexts of interpretation	62
Chapter 3: The self as an object of imagination	66
The self and the corporeal	66
Total reflexivity	72
Play and game	77
Imagination and the stage of play	78
Imagination and the stage of games: unification	85
Imagination and the stage of games: autonomy	86
Freedom and social control	89
The 'I' and the 'me' and novelty	91

Contents

The 'I' and habits	93
The generalized other and the scientific perspective	95
Habits and the self	99
Imagination and the social self	102
Chapter 4: Problems of the self	104
Self-deception	104
Self-knowledge	122
Self-interest and egocentricity	125
Notes	134
Index	145

ACKNOWLEDGMENTS

I want to note, even if I cannot approach a full description of, my indebtedness to Stanley Cavell and Israel Scheffler. They have been and are both my teachers and my friends, and both have given acute criticisms of and beneficial suggestions about this work. I have, I know, not always heeded their good advice, but they have seen this project through twice, and each, each in his own way, has been steadfast in his encouragement and tactful with the occasional nudge. I have been sustained by their intelligence and boundless goodwill.

This work has also benefited from the generosity of a number of others. One of the anonymous reviews of the rough manuscript of this book was, I later learned, written by Martha Nussbaum. Her comments and recommendations were very helpful, and I thank her for them, as I thank my editor, Stratford Caldecott, for his assistance and suggestions. A small section of this material was read at philosophy colloquia at the University of Minnesota and at Western Michigan University, and I am grateful to colleagues in both Minneapolis and Kalamazoo, first for inviting me to visit, and then for offering such stimulating discussion. I am also grateful to the University of Chicago Press for permission to include extracts from G. H. Mead's *Mind, Self, and Society*, edited by Charles W. Morris.

Thanks, finally, to Dennis Senchuk, for philosophical suggestions and much more besides. I trust he knows the extent of my gratitude, but it is good to record a public version of one of its dimensions.

INTRODUCTION

Gilbert Ryle notes that '"mental" is occasionally used as a synonym of "imaginary" . . . [and] there exists a quite general tendency among theorists and laymen alike to ascribe some sort of an other-worldly reality to the imaginary and then to treat minds as the clandestine habitats of such fleshless beings.'[1] Imagining seems the exercise of a paradigmatically mental faculty, and mental images, seen as the vehicles or the products of this exercise, seem prime examples of psychical entities. The imagination is the creative mind, producing its own private objects in its own private realm. It seems independent of, opposed to, the public world of physical objects; it seems the purest exemplar of the mental. Yet Descartes, in drawing the distinction between corporeal and mental substance and in arguing that his essence is conscious substance, that he is a thinking thing, dismisses the imagination as inessential to his mind, his self:

> I remark . . . that this power of imagination which is in one, inasmuch as it differs from the power of understanding, is in no wise a necessary element in my nature, or in [my essence, that is to say, in] the essence of mind; for although I did not possess it I should doubtless ever remain the same as I now am . . .[2]

Of course, Descartes's contention that the imaginative power is inessential to his nature depends both on his conception of himself as a thinking thing and, also, on his analysis of imagination, an analysis which is, in many important features, shared by the empiricists. For Descartes, 'to imagine is . . . to contemplate the figure or image of a corporeal thing.'[3] And the image is not merely *of* a corporeal thing – it is itself corporeal: '. . . imagination, which can only be exercised in reference to corporeal things, . . . requires the presence of a semblance which is truly corporeal, and to which the mind applies itself . . .'[4] Thus, because these images are not mental, imagination cannot possibly be a necessary element in Descartes's essence, since he is a *res cogitans*.

It is somewhat surprising that imagination is so easily separated from a self which is wholly mental. And, though this separation can be seen as a direct result of the claim that images are corporeal, maintaining that they are incorporeal objects wouldn't immediately restore them to a self whose essence is consciousness. This consciousness would direct itself upon the images, would 'view' them, and they would remain external to it, not part of *its* essence.

Although this alienation of the Cartesian self from imagination may be surprising, it would hardly cause universal philosophic dismay. Those who reject Descartes's conception of the self would scarcely worry about this self's relationship to the imagination. And those, such as the behaviorist James B. Watson, who deny the existence of any special power or faculty of imagination must regard as wholly misguided any attempt to propose any relationship between imagination and the self.

But there is resistance to a Watsonian view. Many feel that a denial of mental images is contrary to their own personal experiences; and most of us are not prepared to agree that the concept of imagination should simply be dismissed as one of the 'heritages of a timid savage past'.[5] And not only do we imagine, but our imaginations do seem importantly tied to our selves: our flights of fancy are uniquely *ours*, and it is in our daydreams, our fantasies, that our selves have, if not their freest expression, at least their most unrestrained play. On the other hand, though our inner lives may sometimes seem thus to be the field of our true selves and though these inner lives may seem sufficiently real to us that we immediately reject Watsonianism, our imaginings can be regarded as utterly trivial, as functionless ornaments added to lives which, to persons who, are otherwise complete.

The temptations we can feel to conflicting positions on this issue

Introduction

may in fact draw some of their force from the seductive power of the Cartesian legacy. Although Descartes himself was clear enough in his exile of imagination from the self, our own opacity about the justifiability of this banishment may reflect both our unsettled, and unsettling, relations to dualism and the attraction, when we begin to think philosophically about our personal nature, the dark attraction of a solitary, introspective methodology. We may vacillate between an attachment to and a dismissal of imagination as we are drawn now to a mental, now to a material criterion of personal identity and as we either feel ourselves immersed in our private psychologies or instead find ourselves impressed by our actual conduct, our public behavior. Our attention is focused on a sample self – each of us possesses his or her own exemplar; and as we look more closely at this always available specimen we may shift from embracing a Cartesian view of the self to reacting against it, but we remain riveted by this single case, placing it now here, now there, along a single axis of alternatives.

If we could unfix our gaze from the single case, if we could widen our scope to notice the context in which the individual self is always found, we might add a dimension to our inquiry that would allow us to take more stable bearings. The context we need is the social. And for an illumination of that context, we might well try the resources of philosophical pragmatism.

Pragmatism famously opposes certain habits of the Cartesian tradition: it rejects the idea of intuitive self-consciousness, and it takes continuous inspiration from an animus against a variety of potent dualisms. Perhaps most crucially to our present confoundment, it argues that productive inquiry has a social character. Of course, in the firm grip of Cartesian doubts, we can worry whether we are entitled to claim this new dimension, to assume the social context. It is a curious virtue of pragmatism that it can offer some doctrinal liberation on this very point: theoretical origins need some warrant, but, pragmatism notes, that may come in and through their sequel. It would beg no questions to seek a pragmatic justification for a consideration of the social context of the self. We would then not need to substantiate the propriety of an allegiance to an axiomatic foundation for inquiry; we could instead proceed tentatively, testing the wisdom of our assumptions by careful examination of the consequences of their adoption.

Introduction

With this provisional sense of our beginnings, and with this particular budget of problems – facing the puzzle of the relation between imagination and the self, we immediately encounter deeper bewilderment about the nature of each of the relation's terms – we should certainly explore the views of George Herbert Mead.

Among the leading thinkers of the original movement of American pragmatism, Mead is the one most consistently concerned with the topic of the self. His work has not yet, however, been fully received by philosophy. Even given the recent renewal of interest in pragmatism, and particularly measured against the intensity of attention directed toward Charles Sanders Peirce, William James, and John Dewey, Mead remains a comparatively neglected figure in philosophy. His contention that the self is a social creation and his explanation of and attempts to sustain that contention have, however, earned him an honored place in the discipline of sociology. Introductory texts in that field usually identify him as one of the field's pioneers, and researchers in some realms of that discipline declare his contribution to be more than merely preliminary, his status to be more than that of an important precursor. So, for example, Sheldon Stryker, writing a lead essay for the source book *Social Psychology, Sociological Perspectives*, says that Mead 'is the single most important influence shaping symbolic interactionism . . .'[6] Peter Berger claims that

> [i]t is through the work of George Herbert Mead and the Meadian tradition of the 'symbolic-interactionist' school that a theoretically viable social psychology has been founded. Indeed, it may be maintained that in this achievement lies the most important *theoretical* contribution made to the social sciences in America.[7]

Mead's mature self-identification is, nonetheless, with philosophy, as was, during his lifetime, his settled institutional identification. And it is not in fact sociologists alone who have felt his shaping influence or the power of his theoretical insights. Dewey, writing in 1931, for Mead's memorial service, said of his friend and colleague:

> His mind was deeply original – in my contacts and my judgment the most original mind in America of the last generation. . . . I

Introduction

dislike to think what my own thinking might have been were it not for the seminal ideas which I derived from him.[8]

But Mead sowed his ideas primarily through conversations and lectures. His books were published posthumously, having been assembled from a mix of stenographic records of some of the courses he taught at the University of Chicago, student notes on his classes, his own lecture notes, and his unpublished manuscripts. When that work began to appear in print, in a more or less systematic form, it was roundly applauded. Alfred North Whitehead's response was typical: 'I regard the publication of the volumes containing the late Professor George Herbert Mead's researches as of the highest importance for philosophy. I entirely agree with John Dewey's estimate, a seminal mind of the very first order.'[9] But the ideas of this mind, even if they did germinate and find some expression in the work of a number of colleagues and students, have not really taken root in the history of philosophy.

An adequate description of this fact, and an explanation or a reasoned account of it, would require not just a full survey of Mead's thought, but considerable reflection on the contemporary history and character of, the assorted forces on and within professionalized philosophy. Such a study would be fascinating and could, no doubt, produce insight and wisdom, the kind of self-knowledge which seems natural to the discipline of philosophy, but which it may not always display. This book, however, is not that study.

My focus here is on a set of problems about the self and imagination. I want to untangle some of these perplexities, to weave a coherent new picture of the self and show its relation to a revised conception of imagination. Mead's theories provide a useful framework for this enterprise.

His thoughts carve an advantageous path of entry to these topics because his approach to philosophy is controlled by a number of ideas which happen to provoke a particular tension at the intersection of problems about imagination and the self. He wants to be – claims to be – a behaviorist, but he asserts that any attempt to deny the existence of mind or consciousness or 'to reduce all "mental" phenomena . . . to behavioristic terms . . . is misguided and unsuccessful . . . [and] leads inevitably to obvious absurdities.'[10] He says that 'the psychological datum is best defined . . . in terms of accessibility [and] that which is accessible, in the experience of the individual, only to the individual himself, is peculiarly psychological' (*MSS*, p. 10). Yet in his psychology he advocates 'dealing with experience from the standpoint of society' (*MSS*, p. 1). Hoping to understand the human individual in terms of his or her conduct, but insisting that that conduct can only be understood in terms of the social context in which it appears and functions, Mead develops and applies the methodology of *social behaviorism*. Yet he wants neither to deny nor to ignore the private, the 'mental', or the subjective, so his task is to account for individual psychologies through a study of the social.

Mead's project involves an attempt to demonstrate that 'minds and selves are essentially social products, products or phenomena of the social side of human experience' (*MSS*, p. 1). We know that, proceeding with a Cartesian methodology, the advertence to social interaction can seem an illicitly presumptuous move. But we must note that the social behaviorist has a symmetrical worry: to this theorist, there is an unwarranted assumption spirited into the assertion that the self is simply *given*, an erroneous assumption embodied in the idea that the mind or self cannot be explained by or grounded on something more fundamental. We have yet to measure the importance of the reversibility of this charge of inappropriate supposition. But for now it is worth remembering that it is not, of course, just Descartes who finds himself in a solitary predicament. Egocentric and atomistic methodologies have been the prevailing guides of most philosophic discussions of the person, whether rationalist or empiricist. (This may, in fact, be one reason for, or at least a further indication of, the difficulty the philosophic tradition has had – after the high praise and the hopeful forecasts of his distinguished and generally discerning contemporaries – in assimilating Mead.)

Nonetheless, it is precisely this reversed perspective which I want to explore and, to some extent, exploit. Mead is a crucial figure for any philosophical study contemplating a social genesis of the self; and it seems to me that there is so much that is penetrating, so much that seems correct, in his vision of the self as a social creation, that his account deserves full attention. I think we shall find that Mead's social behaviorism supplies a fresh outlook on some problems about the self: his approach to the nature of the self is, I think, quite plausible, at least superficially;

Introduction

and it is, even upon careful scrutiny and after criticism, deeply helpful. In addition, the constraints of social behaviorism on an account of imagination may turn out to be – though soberingly narrow – bracing, perhaps perversely productive.

I shall, then, in Chapter 1, describe Mead's developmental account of the self. Evolutionary theory exercised a profound general influence on the pragmatists, and so did the new sciences of man. (Indeed, some of the pragmatists, Mead clearly included, themselves contributed to the evolution of the specialized social sciences.) Mead's theory of the self finds its place in a world transformed by the Darwinian revolution: Thus, believing that each human organism must develop in order to have, to possess, a self, and realizing that the type of creature capable of developing a self could have as biological ancestors creatures completely lacking this possibility for growth and refinement, Mead tries to track both an ontogeny and a phylogeny. In both stories, at the crucial point of genesis and in all succeeding elaboration of the self, Mead finds at work a mechanism he calls 'the vocal gesture'. It is the vocal gesture, he claims, which explains, as it contributes to the emergence of, the self's essential characteristic: its reflexivity, its capacity to be an object to itself.

Today it is not uncommon to assert some special connection between language, socialization, and the development of the individual mind or self. So, for example, Rom Harré says that 'language ... [is] the indispensable and unique basis of the psychic community of men',[11] that 'the psychic community of human beings is created by their linguistic powers.'[12] Philosophy has, of course, long believed in a link between language use and a distinctively human mind, but in recent years some relativized and more specifically developmental versions of this belief have gained great currency in the theoretical substrata of work in a variety of fields, from philosophy, to the social sciences, to literary studies. The view has become popular that language does not simply disclose but also enables thought and self-reflection; and it is a widely held conviction, a judgment often traceable to the influence of Wilhelm von Humbolt's classic work or to Edward Sapir and Benjamin Whorf's intriguing hypothesis, that the shared social categories of a native language help constitute the categories of the individual mind, help determine some general dimensions of its particular character and capacities.

Introduction

But if some vague beliefs about the relation between mind, self, society, and language have become common, it is much less common to encounter a detailed attempt to make precise and to argue for the claimed relations. R. S. Peters complains that theories purporting to link the development of mind, or individualized consciousness, to the socializing medium of language fail to face 'the prior problem of how the child comes to take noises as symbols.'[13] I think this complaint is, in general, justified; but Mead does, in fact, attack just this problem, and it is to his straightforward and abiding credit that he offers toward its solution, and toward the larger related questions concerning the connections between language, thought, and the self, more than just suggestive intimations.

His remarks on this problem, these issues, are, once again, foundational for some social scientists. Basil Bernstein, for example, himself noting that even '[i]f we grant the fundamental linkage of symbolic systems, social structure and the shaping of experience it is still unclear *how* such shaping takes place', says that 'Mead is of central importance in the solution of [this] difficulty . . .'; 'Mead outlined in general terms the relationships between role, reflexiveness and speech and in so doing provided the basis of the solutions . . .'[14]

My own view is that Mead deserves considerable honor for delineating clearly the shape of the philosophical puzzle about socialization, speech, and self, but that there are grave flaws in some of the elements he would arrange in solution to the puzzle. After presenting my brief sketch of his account of the self, I shall examine some of those flaws, focusing my criticisms on the crucial theory of the vocal gesture and on the understanding of meaning with which that theory is allied. I contend that the vocal gesture cannot perform the generative feats Mead claims for it. Mead's attempts to construct a naturalistic analysis of the origins of significant symbol use – and his proposals about the mechanisms of those origins – are interesting and worth serious consideration. But I think the self cannot be seen to debouch from the vocal gesture, and we must, in the end, reject Mead's account of the relation between language and the self.

Nonetheless, Mead's theory of the self can be regarded as something akin to a rough map of the topics to be traversed by any explorer of these regions. Thus, while I shall, as I progress in my own study, sometimes alter and sometimes discard features of his account, I take his work to be an important guide to the ultimate destination, a helpful chart of some common pitfalls and some remarkable points of interest in the terrain which must be travelled.

Besides, even if the details of Mead's picture are seen to be faulty, the outline will remain tempting to social science and should remain attractive to philosophy. If we follow that attraction, and if we fill in that outline with a proper understanding of imagination, I think we can produce a more accurate portrayal of the self. I want to argue that the self is an object of imagination, that its essential reflexivity is achieved not in the vocal gesture but through an act of imagination. In order to produce and sustain this argument, I must limn the appropriate understanding of imagination.

The achievement of this design is the goal of Chapter 2. Mead's remarks on imagination will serve only as a point of departure for my discussion; indeed his lines on this topic are both too few and, I think, too slack either to control or to bear any extended discussion. Nonetheless, I want to note and critically evaluate his occasional comments on imagination, because his reflections on this subject are meant to be consistent with his social behaviorism. Thus we can readily see both some of the promise and some of the difficulties of realizing, on this issue, his methodological ideal.

The thinker whose work on imagination I want to lay next to Mead's is Jean-Paul Sartre. This juxtaposition is more natural than is at first sight obvious. As a matter of intellectual history, Mead and Sartre do share the fact of both influence by and reaction (even if often critical reaction) to a number of distinctive figures, including William James and Henri Bergson. More importantly for this study, although perhaps partially as a result, they both want to set themselves apart from the range of standard views on imagination. They embrace neither traditional empiricist, nor rationalist, nor romantic doctrines on imagination. It is their common refusal of these faiths which makes them appropriate confederates, for me, in the development of the conviction I want to articulate. Mead and Sartre are, of course, not much concordant in philosophy; but a survey of their particular congruences on this topic, and the details of their disputes, can help prepare the ground for the view I want to propose. That view will also be built

Introduction

on Wittgenstein's remarks on the phenomenon of 'seeing . . . as . . .'

And it is, in fact, through attention to this latter phenomenon that we may find ourselves able to grant a renewed potency to Mead's methodological vision, his social behaviorism, even as we explore a realm generally supposed beyond that vision's scope. I do not pretend, nor do I want, to offer a behavioristic theory of imagination; nor will I show how the bare capacity to imagine is derived from, or engendered by, complications in the workings of social processes. But I do intend to approach the mystery of imagination in part through its connections to behavior and social interaction, and so I will keep faith with some part of Mead's pragmatic project.

The results of these efforts must then be applied and tested, and so I will return to the theoretical framework which houses Mead's notion of the self. I believe we shall find, however, that the replacement, the displacement, of Mead's central pillar, the vocal gesture, by the new beam of imagination, transforms the whole structure and helps in the building of a rather different, a better conception of the self. In Chapter 3 I shall explicate the meaning and the force of my claim that the self is an object of imagination, that its reflexivity is worked through an act of imagination in which one sees oneself *as* (something or other).

An early point of exposition must touch on the problem of the connection and the distinction between the self and the body. Reflection can be shown characteristically to focus on what might reasonably be called corporeal, or, at least, public – on utterances, deeds, conduct, the movements and shapes and dispositions of the body. I think the body has been too often slighted in philosophic discussions of the self: to begin to do it justice we must say how, in the imaginative act of interpretation, in reflection, if one moves beyond, it is yet still through those corporeal elements and objects.

I must also examine Mead's fairly representative insistence that the self, the mature self, must be understood as an object organized into a 'unity'. His theory of unification is proposed in his remarks on play and games, remarks which have stimulated any number of empirical research projects. I find that while I can endorse the idea that there is a kind of play which is correctly invoked in an account of the nature and the development of the

Introduction

self – play which is a part of childhood, which does contribute to a child's growth in self-awareness, and which does represent the process constitutive of the self – I want to argue that the organizing and unifying function Mead assigns to games is crucially misconceived. The argument I shall offer involves comment on the problems of autonomy, personal freedom and social control, and the function of habits in human lives.

In the course of my disputes with Mead on these topics, I shall also be measuring the gravity of the fact that a whole or complete self does indeed not seem the object of the imaginative act of reflection. I believe, and shall try to show, that this is not evidence of the inadequacy of an account which asserts that imagination is the vehicle of self-possession but, rather, a fact which discloses the particular reality or nature of the self. The whole self may not at once be grasped in imagination, but neither does it stand in need of theoretical unification.

Of course, the view of the self I shall be presenting will not show or explain the self's development from biological or physiological materials alone. (But neither, as we shall see, is that worthy goal of Mead's reached by him.) A form of imagination is central to my story, and I do not trace the development of imagination from biological or physiological materials alone. If I rest content without such a derivation, satisfied in the attempt simply to describe, not really searching for an explanation of the capacity to imagine, it is not because I regard this capacity as an inexplicable, distinctively human spiritual endowment. Whether or not the ability to imagine is a specifically human trait, I shall insist only that we are inhuman if we are without either this ability or the willingness to exercise it.

To further ground this insistence I shall, in Chapter 4, consider the implication of my conception of the self for some affiliated theoretical and practical issues. The problems of self-deception, self-knowledge, self-interest and egocentricity will be placed in the context of this account of the self, and I hope there will be reciprocal illumination. Through the challenge of these problems I want to make clearer the view of the self finally maintained and to suggest that, with that view, we find that the nature of self-deception becomes less obscure, that self-knowledge can be seen as both a task and an accomplishment, and that egocentricity can be deprived of its shadowy claim to be an ineluctable human fate.

Introduction

Most philosophic discussions of self-deception appear as attempts to explain, or explain away, the very possibility of what seems a common yet theoretically vexing phenomenon. I think it will prove useful to shift the focus of discussion, to put aside for a time the obsession with finding an adequate account of the character or state of mind of the self-deceiver, in order to take up an antecedent concern about our identification, and our ascriptions, of self-deception. If we try to discern what provokes the charge of self-deception, we may, guided by our new conception of the self, reach the conclusion that the typical locus of the incoherency of self-deception is not wholly within the individual. Attributions of self-deception may mark points of conflict between an individual's imagination of himself or herself and the community's view of that individual. To explain and sustain the analysis of self-deception suggested by the affirmed account of the self, it will be necessary to study the issues of truth and objectivity in the sphere of the personal.

Thus this analysis of self-deception can intersect some portion of the topic of self-knowledge, and we shall find that the shape of this intersection dovetails interestingly with one small sector of a pragmatic theory of truth. In this area of the personal, the goal of certainty may be supplanted, the ideal of absolute truth dissolved into a vision of a constructed and constructive social harmony. Self-knowledge will then be seen as bound to self-development, and the achievement of self-knowledge will require an activity aimed not at the ascertaining of simple facts, but at complex social validation. I shall argue that imagination plays a cognitive role in self-knowledge; but self-knowledge must be understood as always tinged with affect, as involving both passivity and activity, as being both a function and a modifier of social interaction.

If the new theory of the self suggests radical reinterpretations of self-deception and self-knowledge, it may even allow a refutation of a basic belief about self-interest. A consideration of William Hazlitt's particular version of the notion of sympathetic imagination can set the stage. His theory will be rehearsed, but it will be modified to accord with this work's view of imagination. The result, placed in a context allowing full attention to the claimed social structure of the self, can be used to mount a rejection of an idea of the metaphysical priority of egocentricity: one's connection to one's future is given in imagination, and imagination can thus

Introduction

serve as a foundation for interested action. But one can equally imagine and be moved by the future of another. Indeed, the very mode through which we are attached to ourselves is the mode through which we might fasten to others and their interests: this sympathetic link is forged in the very act of self-reflection. If one apprehends oneself imaginatively, one sees oneself as an object, as another would, and one thus assumes the subjectivity of the other. I shall finally argue, then, that just as imagination can take us to ourselves, it can carry us out of and beyond ourselves, beyond selfishness.

That conclusion seems an appropriate resting place for an exploration of the social aspects of self and imagination. The journey of course begins in company too. It is well to remember that we always and inevitably begin any philosophic quest, no matter how idiosyncratic, in the midst, or in the specific opposition set by the placement, of others – others' texts, others' thoughts. In one of his essays, 'Reality in America', collected in *The Liberal Imagination*, Lionel Trilling remarks that 'a culture is not a flow, nor even a confluence; the form of its existence is struggle, or at least debate – it is nothing if not dialectic.'[15] I want to enter the struggle, situate my debate, with the contentions of George Herbert Mead. Let us turn, then, to Mead's theory.

1
MEAD'S THEORY OF THE SELF

MOTIVATION FOR AND TERMS OF MEAD'S ACCOUNT

Mead holds that the self is distinguished by its reflexivity. Its essential characteristic is its capacity to be an object to itself. The self is thus not the same as the body, for, while the eye can see the foot and the left hand can feel the right, the body can never experience itself as a whole, and it is just this sort of experience which marks the self. But the self is not to be regarded as a Cartesian mind or soul or as a substance or entity simply endowed with this unique capacity. According to Mead, the self is not present in the individual at birth but emerges and develops in and through the life of the physical organism. And the mechanism for this emergence and development can be found in the process of social activity.

A social act is one which involves, implicates, or requires for its completion more than one individual. The act may be constructive or destructive; it may support the lives of the individuals involved or it may hinder or obstruct one or more. An individual or organism engaged in a social act need have no awareness of the fact that he (she, it) is so engaged, need have no consciousness of being involved in a joint or communal enterprise, as Mead thinks the examples of the bee and the ant should remind us. In fact, cognizance of one's place in a shared endeavor or antagonism, appreciation of one's particular and relative position in social conduct, requires or is a form of self-consciousness; and one must certainly have (or be) a self in order to be self-conscious.

It is Mead's contention that he can derive the self from the social process, that he can explain the origin and development of the self using the social process as the sole logical and biological precondition. The social process is then itself to be explained in terms of various fundamental biological conditions, and Mead emerges with a theoretical edge on those who would derive the social process from prior, unexplained selves. Before examining Mead's explanation, however, one must wonder about the axiom of his account. Is there any reason to share Mead's initial presumption that the self is that which can be an object to itself?

Although Mead doesn't argue for his starting point, he does hint at two types of justification, one based on etymology, the other on introspection. The word 'self' does derive from a reflexive pronoun, so Mead can marshall that linguistic fact at the outset: 'the characteristic of the self as an object to itself... is represented in the word "self", which is reflexive, and indicates that which can be both subject and object' (*MSS*, p. 136). His explicit use of introspection to determine the nature of the self ('... I am interested [in] the nature of the self as revealed by introspection ...')[1] is, however, somewhat unexpected, given his claim that he is a social behaviorist. Of course, there is nothing illicit in this use of introspection, nothing incompatible with his behaviorism, if the goal is only to determine what wants an account. And introspection does seem to be limited to that role when Mead says that one finds '... in memory ... an attitude of observing oneself in which both the observer and the observed appear.... [O]ne remembers asking himself how he could undertake to do this ..., chiding himself for his shortcoming or pluming himself upon his achievements' (*SW*, p. 142). Now if one agrees that this description is an accurate summary of some part of one's own experience, or if one believes that the word 'self' just does indicate that which, at the least, can be both subject and object, then one can well be interested in the task that Mead sets himself.

An additional source of interest might be found in a consideration of some features or requirements of rationality. Mead insists:

> The apparatus of reason would not be complete unless it swept itself into its own analysis of the field of experience. . . . [I]t is necessary to rational conduct that the individual should thus take an objective, impersonal attitude toward himself, that he should become an object to himself. For the individual organism is obviously an essential and important fact or constituent element of the empirical situation in which it acts; and without taking objective account of itself as such, it cannot act intelligently, or rationally (*MSS*, p. 138).

The idea that an agent must take account of itself in order to act rationally, together with the assumption that rationality is a characteristic of the entities which we call or to whom we attribute 'selves', provides another basis for the specification of the self as that which is or can be an object to itself. Mead speaks indiscriminately of 'the problem of selfhood' and 'the problem of self-consciousness' because of his conviction that this epistrophe constitutes the essential form of the self. Organisms without selves may be conscious, may be aware of their environment; but insofar as they are unaware of themselves as *in* that environment, insofar as they are not conscious of themselves, they lack a full appreciation of the empirical situation. If truly rational action requires a complete perception of the situation within which one acts, and if complete perception requires taking account of oneself as an element of this situation, and if selves are or belong to entities which are capable of rational action; then there are no selves without or incapable of self-consciousness. Thus, Mead contends that fully rational action is possible only for an individual capable of becoming an object to itself.

Whether or not the capacity for rational action is tied to our conception of the self, and so, whether or not Mead can use such a connection to substantiate his assertion that the self is that which can be an object to itself, the plausibility of there being some link between rationality or, at least, intelligent behavior, and taking an objective attitude toward oneself should provide some motivation to the study of this reflexivity. And along with that inducement, Mead can offer the data of etymology and introspection. It seems, then, that whether or not reflexivity is the defining characteristic of the self, it is a feature which should be noted in any analysis of the self's structure. And Mead offers to explain its origin.

MEAD'S ACCOUNT: PHYLOGENY

As Mead sketches the background of the genesis of the self:

> First of all there is the conversation of gestures between animals involving some sort of co-operative activity. There the beginning of the act of one is a stimulus to the other to respond in a certain way, while the beginning of this response becomes again a stimulus to the first to adjust his action to the oncoming response (*MSS*, p. 144).

This description of the conversation of gestures has its primary place in a phylogenetic story of the human species. Mead believes that beings possessing minds and selves not only arose within, emerged from biological evolution, but may also be explained within that framework. The mechanism for the emergence is the social process, and that process, Mead insists, is generated solely by particular biological, physiological conditions.

> The behavior of all living organisms has a basically social aspect: the fundamental biological or physiological impulses and needs which lie at the basis of all such behavior . . . are impulses and needs which, in the broadest sense, are social in character or have social implications, since they involve or require social situations and relations for their satisfaction by any given individual organism . . .'(*MSS*, p. 227).

While it may be true that all living organisms have needs or impulses which are social in character or implication – many, perhaps most plants and quite a number of simple animals are obvious exceptions[2] – Mead does not need this generalization. It is enough that, at a certain level of complexity, animals do have physiological impulses – those related to nutrition and reproduction, for example – whose expression or satisfaction is social. And it seems clear that, at some point well below the niche of human beings on the evolutionary tree, social acts come to be a ubiquitous feature of animal life. Sexual behavior; the interactions between parent and offspring; the establishment of patterns of dominance; the phenomena of herding, of group attack and defense – any of these can provide the occasion for what Mead calls 'the conversation of gestures'.

Making use of Wilhelm Wundt's delineation of the concept of

the gesture, defining the gesture as 'that part of the social act which serves as a stimulus to other forms [animals] involved in the same social act' (*MSS*, p. 42), Mead points out that such stimulation and responsive adjustment may proceed reciprocally, the beginning of the response to a gesture becoming in turn a stimulus, a gesture. One grazing animal becomes agitated and begins to trot; its movement may stimulate those near to it to flee from their foraging; their flight may then stimulate the first animal, and others, to a gallop; and soon the herd is in full stampede. A lost and endangered lion cub may yelp out of its distress; its mother responds to the sound with an approach and a roar; predators scatter and the cub returns to the safety of the source of the growl. Mead's favourite example of the conversation of gestures is the dogfight:

> The act of each dog becomes the stimulus to the other dog for his response. There is then a relationship between these two; and as the act is responded to by the other dog, it, in turn, undergoes change. The very fact that the dog is ready to attack another becomes a stimulus to the other dog to change his own position or his own attitude. He has no sooner done this than the change of attitude in the second dog in turn causes the first dog to change his attitude. We have here a conversation of gestures (*MSS*, p. 43).

But such a conversation does not imply the existence of a language. Language, according to Mead, involves a set of significant symbols, 'a sub-set of social stimuli initiating a co-operative response' (*MSS*, p. 190). Mead wants to provide an analysis of meaning in terms of response ('the response of one organism to the gesture of another in any given social act is the meaning of that gesture' (*MSS*, p. 67)), and he will promote a gesture to the status of a significant symbol only if it provokes essentially the same response in its maker as in the others implicated in the social act of which the gesture is a part. There is no shared or common response in the dogfight. One dog snarls; the snarl may frighten or provoke the second dog, but these responses are not shared by the first dog. He does not respond with fear or aggression, with turned tail or bared teeth to his own snarl. The conversation of gestures proceeds below the level of language, but it is, Mead says, a process out of which language – and, so, he claims, minds and selves – can develop.

I have indicated that the notion of the conversation of gestures may play an important role in a phylogenetic account of human beings. This is not to suggest that this mode of interaction is supposed limited to the animals we regard as our more primitive ancestors. Indeed, the examples used in illustration should preclude this misunderstanding: dogs and lions, for instance, are not on our evolutionary path of descent. And neither should we assume that only species without language would converse in this way, or that human beings would exhibit, at most, only vestigial remnants of this behavior. A human can react to a glance that was not meant to elicit a response, to a posture or mien not deliberately adopted or intended or expected to produce some effect. If unmindful responses, adjustments, proceed reciprocally, this would count as a conversation of gestures. Again favoring examples of pugnacity, Mead cites boxing and fencing as activities involving alternating readjustments which are made largely without conscious thought or considerations (*MSS, passim*).

But humans can also act with and out of an awareness of the responses their acts will elicit. The fencer who feints in order to prompt a particular parry, one which leaves the opponent open to a fatal thrust, is behaving deliberately, out of a recognition of the opponent's responses, and has, in so behaving, greater control over the outcome of the social act, the match. This kind of behavior thus represents an advance over the conduct constitutive of the conversation of gestures. It allows or entails increased mastery over the social process. And since that process is part of, social acts are partly determinative of, the environment, this kind of behavior makes possible increased dominion by the organism over its environment. A species capable of this sort of control would seem rather likely to survive, given the dynamics of evolution. If the form best suited to the environment will survive, a form able to organize the environment to suit itself has an obvious advantage.

But how is this advantage gained? Even if we see that a species capable of some command over its environment is, in virtue of that capacity, less likely to be extinguished by environmental forces, we still do not have a full account of the emergence of such a species or know how this restructuring of its surroundings is accomplished. The example of the fencer who feints to draw out a parry reminds us of how, at the level of the individual, an awareness of the responses of others can be useful; but the example doesn't make clear how this awareness is achieved.

Mead thinks this achievement has as its basis a *sharing* of the responses of others: the foundation for an awareness of the responses of others is established by one's having those responses oneself. This is what is missing in the conversation of gestures. The dog's bared teeth doesn't frighten or warn himself. He is acting with reference to another, and the responses of that other which his acts or gestures elicit are not drawn forth from himself as well. There seems to be no self-stimulation; or, if there is some, still, these responses are not equivalent to or symmetrical with the responses of the other. It is the sight of the bared teeth which influences the second dog, but the first dog doesn't see this sight and so cannot be influenced by his own act in the same way. But there are, Mead claims, certain gestures which can affect the organism making them as they affect those around this organism. Of central importance is the vocal gesture: 'The vocal gesture . . . assails [the] ears [of the one] who make[s] it in the same physiological fashion as that in which it affects others. We hear our own vocal gestures as others hear them' (*SW*, p. 287). The individual may, then, hearing his (her, its) own vocal gestures, arouse in himself the same responses his gestures are arousing in others who hear them.[3] He may respond to himself as another does, and this common response may, in part, determine or control his next gesture or act, and so shape the course or character of the entire social process.

If we remember that Mead wants to analyze meaning in terms of response and remember, too, that he says language requires shared meanings, we can see why he regards vocal behavior as a medium most suitable for the growth of language. Of course, language does not always begin with vocalization; there can be language use among those incapable, those never having been capable, of speech. Mead grants this, but holds to his contention that language can develop only from gestures which stimulate their maker just as they stimulate those others to whom they are first addressed. Movements of the hand, for example, could be seen by their maker as well as by any spectator and so, on Mead's account, could also serve as a basis for language. Mead notes this:

We may see or feel movements of our hands as others see or feel them, and these sights and feels have served in the place of the vocal gestures in the case of those who are congenitally deaf or blind. But it has been the vocal gesture that has preeminently provided the medium of social organization in human society. It belongs historically to the beginning of the act, for it arises out of the change in breathing rhythm that accompanies the preparation for sudden action, those actions to which other forms must be nicely adjusted (*SW*, p. 287).

Mead clearly is trying to reconstruct accurately an aspect of our phylogeny, or, at least, to offer a credible evolutionary account of the emergence of human language, of human minds and selves. And vocal gestures are plausibly emphasized in this reconstruction, first, because they can be seen as arising from typical, inevitable changes in breathing rhythms. Language is to develop from within some ongoing social activity. While visible hand movements, for example, may or may not be a part of a particular activity, some breathing pattern must support our every act. As one illustration we might picture a group of pre-historic men trying to roll away a boulder blocking access to a cave.[4] The grunts and groans which would naturally accompany their strenuous efforts would form a pattern throughout their struggle and might, indeed, come to structure the exertions themselves. The vocal concomitants of their muscular strains could serve as signals which could help bring the individual efforts into coincidence. One man's cry as he throws himself into his labor might influence another to join that attempt, and the latter's accidentally harmonized push could, in that event, be regarded as a response to the first man's vocal gesture. Such unintentional promptings would erupt here and there, from different members of the group as each continues at the task, so there could be mutual influence and stimulation.

And there might be self-stimulation. If a man responds with renewed effort to the sound of another's exertion, then, since he also hears his own cries, he might so respond to himself. If he does, then he is affecting himself as he affects others; he is sharing their responses, and he is reacting to himself as he might to another, as he might to some object in his environment. Thus the vocal gesture, arising naturally from human activity, could constitute the vehicle for a crucial transition in our evolution.

Man, responding to his own vocal gesture, becomes an object to himself.

MEAD'S ACCOUNT: ONTOGENY

Mead's sketch of our phylogeny, his depiction of the development of the basic elements of language and, with language, the possibility of self-consciousness, of human selves, is supplemented by his delineation of a social psychological ontogeny: '. . . in the development of the individual child, there are two stages which present the two essential steps in attaining self-consciousness. The first stage is that of play, and the second that of game . . .' (*SW*, p. 284). In play the child seems to take different roles: he or she plays (plays at being) mother, father, pirate, policeman. He makes a speech and answers as his mother would; he addresses and responds to his doll as his mother addresses and responds to him. Mead says that such play is the simplest form of being another, but, antedating even this sort of activity, the infant may reproduce the tone of voice and, later, some of the articulate sounds produced by the parents in response to his own cries and gurgles. This behavior is not to be understood as imitation, according to Mead; instead we must recognize that:

> the child is continually exciting in himself the responses to his own social acts. In his infant dependence upon the responses of others to his own social stimuli, he is peculiarly sensitive to this relation. Having in his own nature the beginning of the parental response, he calls it out by his own appeals (*SW*, p. 285).

The adoption of roles in play is interpreted similarly: the child is calling out in himself or herself the responses which might be called out in another – in mother, father, in a pirate or policeman.

This interpretation seems especially appropriate when our attention is turned to another remarkable phenomenon of childhood, the imaginary playmate. The invisible companions invented by a great many children are understood by Mead to involve the constructive organization of responses which might be elicited in other persons, but are clearly being called out in the children themselves. They can carry on discussions with these 'friends' or relate the 'friends'' reactions to particular incidents in their shared days. The imaginary playmate cannot be seen as a product of imitation; the attitudes and responses out of which it is confected are not usually discernible shades of a parent's, a teacher's, an acquaintance's attitudes and responses. It is the child himself who is the other, who is being another for himself.

So in play, conversing with an imaginary companion, as a number of children occasionally do, or playing at being someone or something else, as nearly all children often do, the child exhibits and develops the capacity to be an object in his or her own experience. This is or requires the reflexivity which is at the core of self-consciousness, but Mead says that the child must progress to another stage before he or she can be said to have fully developed a self. The child must not only take the roles of others, respond as others; he or she must also use those responses to organize those various roles into a structured whole. This is what the child does in a game involving others; here, the individual's actions are controlled by his or her organization of the other participant's roles.

> If he plays first base, it is as the one to whom the ball will be thrown from the field or from the catcher. Their organized reactions to him he has embedded in his own playing of the different positions, and this organized reaction becomes . . . the 'generalized other' that accompanies and controls his conduct. And it is this generalized other in his experience which provides him with a self (*SW*, p. 285).

In play the child may shift randomly from one role to another; in the game he assumes, supposes, the roles of the other participants, but doesn't usurp or haphazardly take up those roles. Instead he has a definite position, and this position and his actions in fulfilling it are defined, governed, by his organization of the positions, the actions, the expectations of the other participants. This organization may be specified in terms of rules of the game. These rules furnish a structure within which the role of each individual is determined; they constitute a point of reference against which the appropriateness of particular acts can be understood or assessed.

Such organization provides the unity requisite for a self. While in play the child may, with a whim, slip from one role to another, in the game he or she must be, for example, the first baseman; or, in different games, the goalkeeper, or the forward, or the bank, the dealer, etc. Mead says that the child's organization of the attitudes of all those involved in a game, the organization in terms of which his or her own position is established and defined, constitutes an 'other'. It is not, of course, a particular other – not a parent, a teacher, a real or fictitious acquaintance, and not one or more of the other individuals taking part in the game. The character of this 'generalized other' varies with the social context from which it originates, with the social process of which it is an abstraction; and so, as the child moves from game to game, his position and role, and his sense of himself as fulfilling that role, correspondingly vary.

But the child is not merely a participant in this or that well-defined game. He (or she) is implicated in a much larger social process, and as he comes to interact with the community in which he finds himself, he can organize a more comprehensive generalized other. And the more comprehensive this generalized other is, the more complete and unified is his correlated self. Nevertheless, the full development of an individual's self is always advanced by processes which are already essentially present in the game. The child comes to be engaged in a great range of activities, and he or she must share, organize, and generalize the attitudes and responses of many more individuals than just his or her team or playmates. But the task of selfhood remains structurally the same. As Mead summarizes his understanding of this task:

> This getting of the broad activities of any given social whole or organized society as such within the experiential field of any one of the individuals involved or included in that whole is . . . the essential basis and prerequisite of the fullest development of that individual's self: only in so far as he takes the attitudes of the organized social group to which he belongs toward the organized co-operative social activity or set of such activities in which the group as such is engaged, does he develop a complete self or possess the sort of complete self he has developed (*MSS*, p. 155).

Play and the game may thus be seen as emblematic of all the processes and activities in which, through which, an individual's self is formed and develops. Mead's descriptions of these two types of role-adoption – the play at being another and the rule-governed game or sport – might suggest that he is interested in them principally as illustrations: the slight artificiality of the sharp distinction, the tendentiousness of the arrangement of these childhood pastimes in ordered stages can well be understood as serving an illustrative force. But Mead also believes that he has given an essentially accurate portrayal of the dynamics of the child's progress toward self-consciousness, and that play and the game, as he describes them, really do serve the development of the self. The infant or very young child really does begin by

> taking the attitudes of those about him, especially the roles of those who in some sense control him and on whom he depends. . . . [Later, he] goes over from the play into the game in a real sense. . . . He becomes a something which can function in the organized whole, and thus tends to determine himself in his relationship with the group to which he belongs. That process is one which is a striking stage in the development of the child's morale . . .
> Such is the process by which a personality arises (*MSS*, p. 160).

Nonetheless, whether we regard the descriptions of play and game as representations which typify the processes requisite for the attainment of a self or we accept the empirical accuracy of such an account of child development, we must still wonder what makes such processes or such progress possible. How is an individual able to take up different roles, as in play, or to organise a set of roles so as to guide his or her own conduct, as in the game?

Mead's answer is that these capabilities have as their basis the sharing of responses of others. The child can play at being mother because he can provoke in himself some of the responses which are, or might be, called forth from his mother. And he can play first base in a baseball game because the attitudes of the pitcher, the catcher, the batter, and others are 'present in his own make-up' (*MSS*, p. 151). Our question thus becomes: how is the individual able to share the responses of others? Mead's phylogenetic story supplies his answer, explains the remaining element in his ontogenetic account: it is the vocal gesture which can elicit the shared response. The individual making a vocal gesture hears himself as others do and so can arouse in himself the same response he prompts in others. And so he can engage in play, take part in games, and develop a self.

Thus Mead's ontogeny echoes, if it doesn't recapitulate, his phylogeny. This is, of course, not surprising, as the latter history is constructed to yield a framework within which Mead's view of the modern human being may be appropriately lodged. From a consideration of the nature of the human self, from deliberation about its fundamental features, Mead tries to present a clear rendering of its form and its genesis. He is willing to draw on both empirical data and transcendental arguments in order to support his judgments, judgments which have proceeded from a fixed point of conviction about the nature and requirements of selfhood. As Mead relates his understanding and interpretation:

> The self arises in conduct, when the individual becomes a social object in experience to himself. This takes place when the individual assumes the attitude or uses the gesture which another would use and responds to it himself, or tends to so respond. It is a development that arises gradually in the life of the infant and presumably arose gradually in the life of the race (*SW*, p. 243).

If it is acknowledged that his phylogeny is conjectural, still, Mead does not regard its focal element – the account of the vocal gesture – as the result of casual speculation. The individual is not or hasn't a self unless and until he (or she) becomes an object to himself, and the vocal gesture can be understood to provide for, to make possible, this objectification. This position is central to Mead and so deserves careful scrutiny.

Other features of his theory also raise questions. Even if one agrees that the self is characterized by reflexivity, the particular details of structure proposed by Mead are not entirely obvious. Can play and the game really be shown to generate the developments of reflexivity Mead specifies? And are these specific attainments really required for selfhood? (Why, for example, must a generalized other be constructed? Why is not the person who can take the attitude of various other individuals toward his or her own acts adequately self-conscious?)

But an examination of issues surrounding Mead's portrayal of the details of the constitution of the self would well be deferred. Since it is the basic mechanism of reflexivity which is supposed to promote the depicted structure and its development, that basic mechanism should receive our first attention. We turn, accordingly, to a consideration of the vocal gesture, to an evaluation of the part it plays in Mead's account of the self.

PRELIMINARY CRITICISMS

Mead wants to derive the self from the social process, to demonstrate that the self can arise in the course of natural complications in the social conduct of organisms without selves. But it seems to me that his suggested vehicle of transformation, the vocal gesture, cannot carry that load. One may indeed hear one's own utterances, and let us suppose that an individual can hear his own utterances just as those around him do. It doesn't follow that he has thus become an object to himself. This seems not importantly different from the eye seeing the foot; and if someone is looking down over my shoulder, he sees my foot roughly as I do: yet Mead, in distinguishing the self from the body, cites this very example to represent a relation not marked by the total reflexivity which he says characterizes the self. The eye can see the foot, but we cannot see all of our backs; the hand may touch the back, but then, the hand cannot touch all of itself. So, Mead says, the body does not experience itself as a whole and, hence, must not be identical with the self, which can exercise this comprehensive reflexive grasp. But is the individual hearing his own vocal gesture thereby apprehending himself as a whole? The vocal gesture heard by its maker just as it is heard by others may be an object to its maker; but does that object comprise the self? We may perhaps regard our utterances as *part* of our selves – with words we express ourselves; that is, press ourselves outward – but could any speech constitute the whole of one's self?

Mead lays heavy stress on the possibility that an individual might respond to his or her own utterances as another, as to another. But Mead's emphasis is misplaced, for the realization of this possibility would not engender or secure a self. If my right arm is numb because I have been sleeping on it, I might brush against it with my left hand and be startled by what I momentarily take to be a foreign object. Similarly, if one is an object through and in one's vocal gesture, one is a foreign object – if I actually respond to my own utterance as another would, or as to another, I do not seem to grasp that it is *my* utterance. The man frightened by his own shout would be a comic figure, a person with diminished, and not with developing, self-awareness. If this is the virtue of the vocal gesture, if it allows one to react to oneself as to a foreign object, if it elicits from its maker responses perfectly symmetrical with those prompted in other individuals, then its power seems an obstacle to self-possession. In sum, the self as a unity, as that which experiences itself as a whole, seems not to be generated by the vocal gesture.

But if the vocal gesture cannot explain the emergence of the self, if Mead has failed to show how it could work the required transfiguration of an organism without a self, still, it may be that Mead has highlighted a resource important, indeed vital to the structure of the self, even though not its source. The vocal gesture might be an instrument of objectification for the developed or existent self. And even if an individual experiences only part of himself in hearing his own utterance, still, the vocal gesture might be a device whose employ is crucial as an application of the reflexive capacity.

Sustaining this conception of the importance of the vocal gesture is a continuation of the supposition that an individual hears his own utterance just as those around him do. Can this supposition be maintained? Wittgenstein remarks: 'My own relation to my words is wholly different from other people's.'[5] He thinks it might be said that one does not hear oneself (*PI* II, p. 191), and that 'if I listened to the words of my mouth, I might say that someone else was speaking out of my mouth' (*PI* II, p. 192). This reversal of Mead's position serves as a summary reminder of a number of features of our relations to our words, features which seem ignored or distorted by Mead's theory. I do not normally have to listen to or even hear myself to know that I am speaking, but others do have to listen or hear my voice.[6] I hear another's utterances and perhaps draw conclusions about the speaker from those words and that tone of voice, but 'one does not infer one's own conviction [or one's own doubt, etc.] from one's own words' (*PI* II, p. 191). I do not ordinarily learn of my anger or my satisfaction, my joy or despair by hearing my own words or tone, though another might learn of my attitude or state by or in hearing my words and tone. But it is not merely that one need not hear or listen to oneself as one hears or listens to others.

The homely idiomatic criticisms 'He likes the sound of his own voice', 'He likes to hear himself talk' derive some of their force from a common acknowledgment of the inappropriateness of some acts of listening to oneself as one would to another. These disparagements are used to mark a certain kind of insincerity. They are often applied to the speaker who goes on for too long, but they suggest more than that the speaker is tediously prolix: the discourses of such a speaker are too long – whatever their length – just because his relation to his words is improper. He is not talking primarily to inform, to persuade, to explain, to assure, to question, to answer, to do anything we regard as the fit employ of words. He is talking instead to hear himself talk, and this is unsuitable. It is noteworthy that we so easily recognize the man listening to the sound of his own voice – his mellifluent cadences please him so; his resonant bass strikes him as worthy of rapt attention. And, though we might ourselves have reacted with pleasure or awe to his voice, when it is evident that he shares our reaction, it is evidently unseemly.

'If I listened to the words of my mouth, I might say that someone else was speaking out of my mouth.' This is not only a dramatic way of putting the fact that we do not normally listen to our own words, the fact that we do not hear them and our voices exactly as our auditors do and so might not even recognize our voices if we really did hear them as others do, (as is evidenced by the surprise we often feel when we first hear ourselves on tape). It is also a declaration that listening to oneself could constitute a mode of self-alienation. Since we only listen to others, if I listened to myself, I would be an other to, estranged from, myself. This is essentially the point I urged above, against Mead: although he may be right in suggesting that the vocal gesture could allow one to become an object to oneself, one would thus be a foreign object. The issue above was, however, Mead's contention that the self as a unified whole could be generated by the vocal gesture. But we can now also note, shifting our attention from the question of the emergence of the self to a consideration of the developed individual, that the person who listens to his or her own words is stained by this rupture of the self. Imagine a very personal attestation – for example, a statement that one is in love. The man who hears, *listens* to himself say 'I love you' would seem to be inappropriately distanced from his words. It seems such an avowal could not be whole-hearted; the man is not entirely behind his words. As another example, think of the possibility of reading aloud a page of prose and coming to hear, as if from the outside, the words one is forming. This can happen if one becomes absent-minded, if the reading becomes automatic, if one is not attentive to the sense of the passage being recited. Such an occurrence is disconcerting; a common consequence of the realization that one is thus hearing one's own reading is the loss of one's place in the text. There is often a slight difficulty in resuming one's composure as a speaker – one has lost track of what one was saying. It is as if the paths of speaker and listener are always separate, though covering the same course; and one cannot maintain one's footing on both paths simultaneously.

If it is unusual to listen to one's own words, if it can be seen to be sometimes obstructive and sometimes improper to hear and respond to or be moved by one's utterances as if their source were another, why does Mead want to insist that it is only through hearing one's own vocal gestures that one can develop or possess a self? Part of the answer to this question, part of the motivation for his neglect of or obliviousness to these facts about our relations to our words, can be found in the distorting influence of his view of meaning. We may recall that Mead hopes to provide an analysis of meaning in terms of response. It is his judgment that

> Much subtlety has been wasted on the problem of the meaning of meaning. It is not necessary, in attempting to solve this problem to have recourse to psychical states, for the nature of meaning . . . is found implicit in the structure of the social act, implicit in the relations among its three basic individual components: namely, in the triadic relation of a gesture of one individual, a response to that gesture by a second individual, and a completion of the given social act initiated by the gesture of the first individual (*MSS*, p. 81).

To convince us that meaning should not be regarded as a 'psychical state', or as a content of mind or consciousness, Mead tries to show that rudimentary meaning can be found in, for example, the conversation of gestures, though the organisms involved are not taken to be communicating ideas. One dog snarls and the second, in response, flattens his ears and bares his teeth. The second dog has, without conscious thought, interpreted the first dog's act as a hostile one; the first dog's snarl – which meant an attack was imminent – has initiated a dogfight. 'Response on the part of the second organism to the gesture of the first is the interpretation – and brings out the meaning – of that gesture, as indicating the resultant of the social act which it initiates' (*MSS*, p. 80).

But with language there is conscious communication. A set of symbols is employed to convey meaning. Meanings must be shared for this sort of communicability, so, as Mead tries to maintain his behavioristic framework, he concludes that language requires shared responses. So a vocal gesture, if it is a significant symbol, if it is used for conscious communication, if it is part of a true language, must elicit the same response in its maker as it does in those to whom it is addressed.

I do not propose here a close examination of Mead's account of language except insofar as that account and his remarks on meaning bear directly on his portrayal of the self. But it must be noted that Mead himself finds it impossible to sustain the notion that meaningful utterances must, as a rule, provoke the same response in speaker and hearer. Although he begins by claiming that '[the] vocal gesture becomes a significant symbol . . . when it has the same effect on the individual making it that it has on the individual to whom it is addressed' (*MSS*, p. 46), the shared response is soon reduced to a mere tendency:

> The meaning of what we are saying is the tendency to respond to it. You ask somebody to bring a visitor a chair. . . . The response to the vocal gesture is the doing of a certain thing, and you arouse that same tendency in yourself (*MSS*, p. 67).

And if Mead still seems to be clinging to the possibility of a neat behavioristic reduction of meaning, if this talk of a 'tendency to respond' still seems to promise an account in terms of overt action, hope must be lost when Mead describes the speaker's response as 'implicit'.

> Gestures become significant symbols when they implicitly arouse in an individual making them the same responses which they explicitly arouse, or are supposed to arouse, in other individuals, the individuals to whom they are addressed . . . (*MSS*, p. 47).

But this concept of an 'implicit response' is never clarified, and if an implicit response is just to be understood as precisely not being found in conduct, then the behavioristic account of meaning is not altogether successful. Moreover, the perfect symmetry of speaker and listener, the symmetry which was a prime desideratum because it was supposed to mark the achievement of the objectification of the self – the speaker hearing and responding to himself exactly as another – that symmetry of position and role is conspicuously eroded.

This deficiency of symmetry would seem to have serious consequences for Mead's account of the self, as his dependence on an equivalence is heavy. Genuine sharing by the speaker of the listener's response is to constitute access to the standpoint of another; and this standpoint is to provide, in turn, the position – a position outside the self – which allows self-awareness. And self-awareness makes possible self-governance and, through self-governance, increasing control of the social process. As Mead recounts the interconnections of these possibilities:

> Where the response of the other person is called out and becomes a stimulus to control [a man's] action, then he has the meaning of the other person's act in his own experience. . . . [The vocal gesture involves] an arousal in the individual himself of the response which he is calling out in the other individual, a taking of the role of the other. . . . One participates in the same process the other person is carrying out and controls his action with reference to that participation (*MSS*, p. 73).

An example selected by Mead makes plausible this outline of the dynamics of self-control and social adjustment. (See *MSS*, p. 65.) Again emphasizing the special importance of the vocal gesture, Mead points out that one can hear oneself speaking in, for example, an irritated tone of voice and so catch and curb that quality. But a facial expression of irritation, though likely to affect those others with whom an individual is in immediate commerce and, thus, to affect the tenor of the social intercourse itself, is unlikely to be noticed by the irritated person himself. An individual – such as an actor or a ballet dancer – who is particularly interested in gaining control over his own facial gestures, his own countenance and physical appearance, might well use a mirror in his training. The mirror allows him to see himself, to see the change made when he relaxes one muscle, the impression produced when he tightens another. If he is to use his body consciously as an instrument of expression and communication, it seems he must come to be aware of the effects his appearance and movements will make. The mirror aids his access to these effects. Seeing himself as others will helps him achieve the self-command, the physical mastery, which will allow him to control his performance for others. If we think once again of Mead's irritable individual, we realize that even if he is or becomes aware of his own tensed jaw and narrowed eyes, unless he also knows what an unpleasant visage he thus presents, he may not comprehend or be able to modify the effect on others of his tensed face, his irritated expression. It does seem that this sort of self-governance and this sort of social accommodation depend on somehow attaining a position outside the self.

But if the actor and the ballet dancer in using mirrors are trying to see themselves as others will, are they also seeking to respond as others? If we grant that an individual speaking in an irritated tone can hear himself – and, despite what I have said about the asymmetry of speaker and listener, against Mead's unqualified claim that we hear ourselves just as others do, still, I do not of course deny that we can hear ourselves talk – do we grant that that person must respond as another in order to alter his socially abrasive voice? The dancer whose perfected jetés will draw breathless gasps from the audience should certainly not share this reaction. (If the dancer *does* become breathless, the audience will not.) Those listening to the irritable person may be frightened or antagonized by his tone, but, even when he hears and so checks himself, he has not usually frightened or antagonized himself. If hearing his own vocal quality prompts him to change his tone, it may be because he perceives the reaction it will provoke, but it does not seem he is made aware of this reaction by having it. Mead tries another illustration: 'One starts to say something, we will presume an unpleasant something, but when he starts to say it he realizes it is cruel. The effect on himself of what he is saying checks him . . .' (*MSS*, p. 141). But if cruel words hurt another, surely they do not (or do not straightforwardly or do not in the same way) hurt the individual who utters them. One who stops speaking because he realizes that what he is saying is brutal, that his words will sting, has not stung himself. It is not 'the effect on himself of what he is saying' that checks him, but his sensitivity to the effect of what he is saying on others.

Mead seems on the brink of acknowledging this truth, or to be writing under the force of its influence, when he says that conscious communication is distinguished by the fact that the participants are constantly responding to the meaning of their own utterances. (See, e.g., *MSS*, p. 67.) But this claim not only casts another cloud over his attempt to explain meaning in terms of response; it is also a defective emendation, an as yet inadequate recognition of the complexity of social interaction. The original explication of meaning seems obscured, for it was proposed in an effort to reduce meaning to behavior, to response: conscious communication was to involve shared responses to a gesture or utterance. But when Mead now characterizes conscious communication as requiring of the participants not shared responses to utterances, but responses to the meanings of utterances, then either his behavioristic analysis of meaning is given up as patently inadequate – for the analysandum stubbornly recurs – or this characterization is a refinement of his account, and Mead is saying that conscious communication demands responses to shared responses. The confusion of his position is evident when he declares that

> the significant gesture or significant symbol . . . calls out in the individual making it the same attitude toward it (or towards its meaning) that it calls out in the other individuals participating with him in the given social act, and thus makes him conscious of their attitude toward it (as a component of his behavior) and enables him to adjust his subsequent behavior to theirs in light of that attitude (*MSS*, p. 46).

But if any dependence on a notion of meaning not analyzable in terms of response immediately darkens Mead's behavioristic project, the other alternative, adherence to the idea that conscious communication requires of the participants responses to shared responses, is not ultimately illuminating. We have already seen, in part by looking more closely at the very cases offered by Mead as illustrations, that the speaker who modifies his or her words or tone in response to or in anticipation of the reaction of the listener does not ordinarily share the listener's reaction. One is not antagonized by one's own irritable utterance, and one is not oneself crushed by a cruel criticism addressed to another.

Furthermore, it is not merely that the speaker normally happens not to have the same response as the listener; it must also be recognized that if the speaker were himself really to respond as others do, then he would not be said, in that response, to have got outside himself. Mead suggests that the sharing of the other's response allows one access to the other's standpoint, secures for one a point outside the self from which the self may be viewed as an object. But one has not found one's way to the viewpoint of another if one simply happens to respond to an utterance as he or she does. The shared response cannot, in itself, constitute a mode of access to another: suppose a man alarms himself as well as others by his shout; insofar as he is genuinely alarmed, insofar as alarm is actually *his* reaction, that reaction surely cannot be cited as particularly definitive of the position of one who would be an other to him.

Mead might try to resist this criticism by insisting that the shared reaction, though of course not determinative of the 'otherness' of the other, is nonetheless part of, partly constitutive of the other's position. So, he might conclude, to the extent that one does share the other's reaction, to that extent one has in fact discovered the viewpoint of another. But surely discovery requires something more or other than this. A man could find the mold of penicillia in his bread box without thereby discovering penicillin; until he began to notice the connection between the fungi and the inhibition of bacterial growth, his possession of a green loaf would be absolutely irrelevant to the discovery of the antibiotic. And having the same response as another does not guarantee, and certainly does not constitute, access to or discovery of the other. One must see the connection between, the identity of, one's own and the other's responses in order for this sharing to be relevant to even a limited discovery of the viewpoint of the other.

We may conclude, then, that the shared response is neither necessary nor sufficient for either establishing a position outside the self or providing access to the attitudes of another. An account of these accomplishments must lie elsewhere, and it is in pursuit of that account that I will want to explore some problems about the nature and function of imagination. To clear a path toward those topics, however, a few more features of Mead's theory of language must be examined.

It may be recalled that the discussion of the shared response was occasioned by the thought that Mead's allegiance to this notion, his placement of it at the center of the view of meaning in his theory of language, works a distortion in his description of the individual's relation to his or her own utterances. We can now note that Mead's emphasis on the shared response also distorts his portrayal of the individual's relations to others. More precisely, he is led to neglect the individuality, the 'otherness', of the other. This neglect is manifest in his assumption that the adventitious duplication of the other's response embodies access to the other. But, of course, this assumption is wrong, for a common response could be evoked in individuals who are and remain wholly ignorant even of each other's existence. At another level, however, Mead's neglect can be seen as the product of attention to certain patterns of social life, can remind us of a particular failure often found in human relationships. We do ourselves often neglect alterity, or acknowledge it most inadequately, preferring to suppose that its recognition is no special task and that response for it draws along no special burdens. And a form this practical neglect can take just is assuming that one's reactions are shared by an individual with whom one is in commerce, thus constructing for and out of oneself a person who is not the – or even an – other.

Not only does Mead fail to confront the facts and the problems of alterity, but he also disregards certain elements present and influential in social interaction. In particular, he wants to dismiss as inessential to communication all that he relegates to the realm of affect. Although he has, once again, the pursuit of an account of meaning as his motive, the lengths to which he goes in his assertion of a questionable distinction between the cognitive and the affective seem oddly misdirected, given his location of the development of language within a framework of response and social control. Mead remarks that the actor and the poet may play upon, may consciously attempt to arouse the emotions of others. But, he says, '[a] great deal of our speech is not of this genuinely aesthetic character' (*MSS*, p. 148), and, moreover, '[i]t is not a natural situation; one is not an actor all of the time' (*MSS*, p. 147).

Mead places the actor and the poet outside the natural situation of language because, clinging to the idea that consciousness of the import of one's expressions to another requires sharing the other's response, he realizes that, ordinarily, the hostile person does not frighten himself and the grieving individual cannot arouse self-sympathy. Thus, he concludes, except for the special case of artists, who must, he insists, achieve their goals by duplicating their audience's reactions, affective elements cannot form a part of conscious communication.

> What is essential to communication is that the symbol should arouse in one's self what it arouses in the other individual (*MSS*, p. 149).

> On the emotional side, which is a very large part of the vocal gesture, we do not call out in ourselves in any such degree the response we call out in others as we do in the case of significant speech. Here . . . we must know what we are saying, and the attitude of the other which we arouse in ourselves should control what we do say. Rationality means that the type of the response which we call out in others should be so called out in ourselves, and that this response should in turn take its place in determining what further thing we are going to say and do (*MSS*, p. 149).

An assumption that emotions are beyond the bounds of rationality seems at play here, but it is a strained and impoverished picture of human interaction which would allow that *any* affective response is always as likely as another, that no expectations about affective reactions could regularly serve as guides to what we should 'say and do' and, also, that no emotional response actually aroused in the other, if we do not also feel it, could – should reasonably be expected to – 'take its place in determining what further thing we are going to say and do.' Mead's commitment to this picture binds him, then, either to deny that emotions and mood are operative in ordinary conscious communication or to characterize as slightly inauthentic, as a matter of 'acting', any conversation in which the participants are sensitive to and guided in their speech and actions by the feelings of their fellows. This seems an unfortunate conception of human interaction; and against this idea, which encompasses the judgment that we have access to the point of view of another if we merely use and understand the same words he or she does, we might place

Wittgenstein's remark that

> ... one human being can be a complete enigma to another. We learn this when we come into a strange country with entirely strange traditions; and, what is more, even given a mastery of the country's language. We do not *understand* the people (*PI*, II, p. 223).

But if Mead errs in assuming that understanding another's words constitutes achieving the viewpoint of that other, and if this error is compounded by his willful neglect of the place of emotion and mood in human interaction, still, his attraction to the vocal gesture, the word, as a sufficient vehicle of selfhood should not be disregarded. He may misdescribe our verbal interactions with others and misconstrue our relations to our words, but the idea that words are the medium required for the emergence, the existence, of selves should not be lightly dismissed. Words do seem to have creative power, and not just for God and the magician.

Mead says that

> [t]he social process, as involving communication, is in a sense responsible for the appearance of new objects in the field of experience of the individual organisms implicated in that process. Organic processes or responses in a sense constitute the objects to which they are responses; that is to say, any given biological organism is in a way responsible for the existence (in the sense of the meanings they have for it) of the objects to which it physiologically and chemically responds. There would, for example, be no food – no edible objects – if there were no organisms which could digest it. And similarly, the social process in a sense constitutes the objects to which it responds, or to which it is an adjustment (*MSS*, p. 77).

We can grant, e.g., that the stars in the heavens do not depend on man for their existence, but insist that the constellations do. Cygnus, Ursa Major, Ursa Minor, Cepheus were not always there, waiting to be named. They were constituted as objects by the power of our symbols.[7] It seems possible, then, too, that human selves – and some of the particular refinements of attitude and feeling which can be had by the self-conscious human individual – might depend for their emergence on, or might exist only in the context of, language.

Furthermore, it is undeniable that language does provide access to the other's viewpoint and so serves the goal of reflectivity or reflexivity. It is undeniable that the utterances of the other are guides to or must be reckoned in any rendering of the other's perspective.

What is denied is Mead's account of the relation between language and the self. His fundamental claims – that words or significant symbols require shared responses, that the shared response guarantees access to the viewpoint of the other, and that the self is thus generated by the vocal gesture – are faulty. But his approach to the problem of the nature of the self is still attractive and his conviction that the self is a product of the social process still seems sound. So even if we must reject the details of Mead's description of the vocal gesture as the vehicle which carries organisms without selves to self-consciousness, still, we might want to preserve the larger framework of his account.

I would like to suggest that Mead's view of the development of the self in fact depends on the organism's imaginative capacity, that it is only in and through imaginative identification with the other that one can become an object to himself. It might well be thought, however, that this sort of reading of Mead's description of the self's genesis would be so antithetical to his general program that if his account cannot be made to stand without this introduction of imagination, the account must be allowed to fall. Unless the capacity to imagine can be shown to be derived from the workings of the social process – and I don't think it can – it might seem to be a natural endowment which is unexplained and inexplicable and which vitiates any reference to social conduct in an explanation of the self. Mead expresses a sharp distrust of the appeal to native capacities and a strong disappointment with theories of the self which depend on such appeals. In rejecting Charles Horton Cooley's social psychology he notes that in Cooley's doctrine:

> all social interactions depend upon the imaginations of the individuals involved, and take place in terms of their conscious influences upon one another in the processes of social experience. Cooley's social psychology . . . is hence inevitably introspective, and his psychological method carries with it the implication of complete solipsism: society really has no

existence except in the individual's mind, and the concept of the self as in any sense intrinsically social is a product of imagination (*MSS*, p. 224 fn.).

Although this assessment of Cooley's position is accurate, it seems to me that the difficulties in his theory lie not so much in his references to imagination as in his view of it. Cooley's sociological theory as a whole is essentially individualistic; he simply presupposes individual minds, minds enlivened by complex personal ideas, and then tries to study the modifications and developments of these presupposed minds as they are positioned together in society. In Cooley's view, 'society . . . is a relation among personal ideas . . .':[8]

> Society exists in my mind as the contact and reciprocal influence of certain ideas named 'I,' Thomas, Henry, Susan, Bridget, and so on. It exists in your mind as a similar group, and so in every mind. . . . I conclude, therefore, that the imaginations which people have of one another are the solid facts of society . . .[9]

But Mead doesn't find such imaginings sufficiently solid. They cannot, he remarks, be the foundation for some standing natural science, subdivisions of entomology, for example:

> . . . the supposition that the social process presupposes, and is in some sense a product of, the mind seems to be contradicted by the existence of the social communities of certain of the lower animals, especially the . . . social organizations of bees and ants, which apparently operate on a purely instinctive or reflex basis, and do not in the least involve the existence of mind or consciousness in the individual organisms which form or constitute them (*MSS*, p. 224).

Even more crucially, if society is constituted as a function of mind, then the social account of mind and self seems to dissolve. Mead says that although Cooley wants to maintain that 'the self presupposes experience', since experience 'is for him primarily internal and individual rather than external and social, he is committed in his psychology to a subjectivistic and idealistic, rather than an objectivistic and naturalistic, metaphysical position' (*MSS*, p. 224).

But it may be an objective, natural fact that we humans have, along with the opposable thumb and the capacity for upright locomotion, some power of imagination. It is only the description and the placement of such a fact which would disclose or engender a disagreeable commitment to a subjectivistic, an idealistic, or a solipsistic metaphysical position. Cooley says that '... Imagination ... is the *locus* of society.'[10] But if that judgment is reversed, reversed not just logically, but ontologically, if the claim is that society is the locus of imagination, then Mead might be brought to welcome the explicit invocation of imagination to his account of the self. To prepare for such an invocation, to see if an appropriate understanding of imagination is available, let us first consider Mead's remarks on this topic.

2

IMAGINATION

MEAD ON IMAGINATION

A behaviorist account of imagination may not seem a likely prospect. Imagination seems to have no natural behavioral manifestations, no signs, no symptoms. Mead regards imagination as something 'mental' – he says that the 'content of . . . minds is (1) inner conversation . . . [and] (2) . . . imagery' (*MSS*, p. 190 fn.) – and he insists that any attempt to reduce mental phenomena to behavioristic terms will fail, will lead 'inevitably to obvious absurdities' (*MSS*, p. 10). It might seem, then, that Mead is bound to develop a metaphysical dualism in the accommodation of images. It looks as if he might be content to offer images (and inner conversation) a separate home of their own – the mind. But this preliminary appraisal is unsettled by Mead's remark that imagery can and should be studied 'in relation to the behavior in which it functions' (*MSS*, p. 190 fn.).

The assumption that imagery does function in behavior is not a common one. It is part of what Mead requires to claim for himself a 'more adequate' (*MSS*, p. 2) behaviorism than that espoused by John B. Watson. Watson seeks to explain the human individual and experience in terms of observable behavior. Because he, along with so many, finds no clear behavioral manifestations of images, he is moved to deny the existence of images and to dismiss the usefulness of any concept of imagination. But Mead is unwilling to deny imagination, and, though he thinks any attempt to reduce imagination to behavior will be unsuccessful, he hopes his theoretical orientation[1] overcomes this benighted feature of Watsonism.

> I want to point out . . . that even when we come to the discussion of such 'inner' experience, we can approach it from the point of view of the behaviorist, provided that we do not too narrowly conceive this point of view. What one must insist upon is that objectively observable behavior finds expression within the individual, not in the sense of being in another world, a subjective world, but in the sense of being within his organism. Something of this behavior appears in what we may term 'attitudes,' the beginnings of acts. Now, if we come back to such attitudes we find them giving rise to all sorts of responses (*MSS*, p. 5).

Mead contends that imagery often serves to call out, or contributes to the calling out of specific responses. In addition to alluding to attitudes which determine acts, Mead also cites some specific examples of imagery provoking responses: reading a printed page – where the individual's glance touches each line of print perhaps only twice, and imagination fills out what is actually seen – and seeing a friend from a distance – where a few familiar features are seen (the posture, the shape of the face, for example), and many more are filled in by imagination. We are abruptly reminded of these contributions of imagery when, for example, we realize we have missed misprints in a text or we meet the distant person and find out our friend but a stranger.

If imagery plays this role, this might suggest a particular understanding of its nature. Mead takes as a consequence of his examples that:

> a considerable part of our perceptual world, the world existing 'out there,' as we say, is made up out of mental images, the same stuff that comes before us in revery, only in that case we are looking at it from the point of view of imagination. These images actually go to make up objects we see and feel.[2]

Although it might seem that Mead is thus committed to regarding the world 'out there' as merely phenomenal or, at least, to

Imagination

maintaining that we experience no more than phenomena, taking him to accept such doctrines would leave his attraction to behaviorism quite a puzzle. Mead in fact repudiates such doctrines. His purpose in insisting that images 'go to make up' the objects of our public world seems instead to be to break down the idea that images are, in any substantial way, in consciousness.

He wants his remarks to show that 'You cannot . . . cut off any particular field of content in our ordinary experience of the world and say, ". . . This is a certain stuff which belongs inside of my head and not to the world"' (*MT*, p. 398). Although many people have thought that an image must be a thing categorically different from an object in the shared physical world, that have thought

> imagery would be not the object, but some copy of the object; not the past event, but some memory of the past event; not future conduct, but a picture of future conduct; [and many have then said that the] image . . . is in consciousness, . . . you cannot say that the image is not in the objective world, for many of them are (*MT*, p. 396).

This is, then, part of an attempt to deny the mind any special set of proprietary objects, any special entities which must be housed in it: what might have been thought the prime examples of entities in consciousness, mental images, are, according to Mead, often in the objective world.

However, some of the support Mead tries to offer for this position presents a rather different point. Objects of imagination can be 'as real as . . . objects of perception', but, he explains, we call certain 'sensuous contents' 'imagery' 'because the objects to which they refer are not the immediate occasions of their appearance' (*MSS*, p. 340): what characterizes imagery 'is its appearance in the absence of the objects to which it refers' (*MSS*, p. 346). Mead is here maintaining his contention that the object of imagination is often in the world, not in consciousness, but his comment further suggests that when I imagine my friend's face on the stranger's form, the objects referred to in my imagery are *not* in or on the present stranger but in or on my friend, who is absent. That is, my images refer to the real, public world, but to parts of it which are not present to me. Thus Mead again claims that images need not be understood as private entities lodged in the mind or consciousness: '. . . the image, in so far as it has objective reference, is not

Imagination

private or psychical' (*MSS*, p. 340). My image of Pike's Peak refers to the mountain in Colorado, not to a copy or picture of the mountain in my consciousness.

But what of images of Pegasus or the Golden Mountain? If it is only 'objective reference' which obviates placing images in the category of the 'private or psychical' and which helps to secure the possibility of a behavioristic account of imagination, then the behavioristic program seems either shortsighted – unmindful of the abundant examples of imagination beyond the objects of heaven and earth – or admittedly, but still unacceptably, partial or limited in its scope. Mead in fact doesn't recognize any problem concerning images of the never-real, concerning 'sensuous contents' which have no objects to which they refer, and I think one explanation of his equanimity is the fact that he has intertwined in his account two different notions of reference. He says:

> As the perceptual sensuous experience is an expression of the adjustment of the organism to stimulation of objects temporally and spatially present, so the images are adjustments of the organism to objects which have been present but are now spatially and temporally absent. These may merge into immediate perceptions, giving the organism the benefit of past experience in filling out the object of perception; or they may serve to extend the field of experience beyond the range of immediate perception, in space or time or both; or they may appear without such reference, although they always imply a possible reference, i.e., we hold that they could always be referred to the experiences out of which they arose if their whole context could be developed (*MSS*, p. 340).

This seems to suggest that we could refer my image of Pegasus to, e.g., some past experiences of wings and a horse; and if Mead suggests this as a mechanism of imagination, he is, after all, clearly in line with most traditional accounts:[3] the image seems to be a copy, a trace, or a decayed version of a sense perception. But pulling out this thread from tradition creates a snarl for Mead. He says that the reference of an image can always be specified by pointing to the perceptual experiences from which it is derived, and that images are of objects once present but now past. But one consequence of taking this view of reference is that when I claim to have an image of my friend now in Paris, the reference of my image cannot be to my friend as he is, now, in Paris; the reference must be said to be some past experience of my friend, e.g., seeing my friend in Cambridge in 1976.

Although such a consequence may not be objectionable to everyone, it is difficulty to see how Mead could square it with his explicit statement that '[imagery's] reference to the future is as genuine as [its reference] to the past' (*MSS*, p. 344). This is an especially difficult issue for him, since he insists that the future is always novel; how can one's image genuinely refer to this novel future if it arises with reference to a determined past, if the very notion of the reference of an image is explicated in terms of the indication of past experience?

And what has become of Mead's claim that imagery is in the objective world? He seems to have slipped from the position that images make up objects in the public world to the view that the objects of images are in the world, and then to have entangled this second view with the contention that images are always to be referred to past perceptions, that the referent of an image is always an object as experienced in the past. There is certainly at least the appearance of internal incompatibilities in his description of imagination, as he moves from saying that the 'world existing "out there"' is made up of images to saying that images are simply 'adjustments of the organism'. To understand what could have prompted such apparently inconsistent remarks and to see what might be salvaged from them, let us consider how some of these convictions could be and have been controverted.

SARTRE COMPARED WITH MEAD

The account of imagination proposed by Jean-Paul Sartre provides a helpful point of comparison. Many of Sartre's claims about images and imagination are strikingly similar to Mead's and seem products of a related animus against prevailing views on these subjects. And the differences between Sartre and Mead seem well worth studying, for, in addition to highlighting difficult and interesting issues, these differences can produce a special puzzle. They are often most robust when Mead and Sartre are trying to support identical convictions. Remarks on the relation between perception and imagination establish a central controversy.

Imagination

As we have seen, Mead claims that our perceptions are often mixed with, filled out by, our imaginings. Jean-Paul Sartre insists that perceiving and imagining are necessarily distinct and incompatible – 'the image is a consciousness which is *sui generis*, which can in no way form a part of a larger consciousness.'[4] Sartre takes his conclusion to follow immediately from phenomenological reflection, but Mead, too, has appealed to a consideration of our ordinary experience. It is noteworthy that each philosopher then enlists his conclusion in the same service: these evidently irreconcilable results are both thought to aid the demonstration that images are not in consciousness. Of course, they each follow different paths to this common destination.

Mead's general program involves redrawing the line traditionally separating the subjective and the objective, recasting the circumstances in which the separation might be thought evident in order to show that what has been supposed homeless without some shelter in a mind (images, sensations, etc.) can as well be lodged in the public, objective world. Sartre's view is that when we recognize the great natural gulf between perceiving and imagining, we will be less inclined to accept an account of imagining which derives its terms from cases of perception. If we have thought visualizing to be a kind of seeing, then, since seeing requires the presence of some object seen, we might think visualizing requires the presence of the object visualized. And, since when I now visualize Pike's Peak, Pike's Peak is certainly not present to me, it must be that some likeness is present; some copy of Pike's Peak must be here – in my mind. But if, on the other hand, we admit Sartre's claim that perceiving and imagining are utterly different, we may not be tempted by the model of perception, may not be seduced into a confidence in the mental image as an object in consciousness. Now from which side, if either, can this theory that images are not contents of consciousness draw its best support? Whose position is more tenable – Mead's or Sartre's?

One might be reluctant to accept Mead's view because the examples he cites seem only tendentiously to be called cases of imagination. One might argue that that is just the way perception functions – perhaps we don't *have* to trace every letter with our eyes in order to actually *see* the line of print. And perhaps if we were as circumspect as we ought to be, we would admit that we don't *see* the image of our friend's face on the distant stranger's form. We don't even *seem* to see a likeness of our friend's face. When we perceive a man from this distance, *all* we see is the shape of the head, the posture, etc. We might immediately *infer* from what we've seen that this fellow we perceive is our friend, and we might then approach him with what turns out to be an inappropriate familiarity; but that doesn't mean we have actually seen an image on the stranger's face, that we have understandably relied on some objective imagery. Mead's examples seem uncompelling.

But, of course, a rejection of Mead's position doesn't entail an acceptance of Sartre's. We haven't produced the premises of a disjunctive syllogism, so no conclusion can be accepted until we have examined Sartre's claims more directly. This examination is undertaken, then, not just to clarify the dispute between Mead and Sartre, but also to focus further attention on the problems which have provoked their contending claims.

SARTRE ON IMAGINATION

We have noted Sartre's insistence that the image presents itself to reflection in such a way that confusion between image and perception is impossible.[5] Because the distinction between image and perception should be evident, given with immediate and absolute certainty, no argument for it is supposed to be required. Nonetheless, Sartre does offer a number of examples and reminders in order to elicit our acknowledgment of this distinction and to make explicit what this acknowledgment implies.

If we examine the situation in which I, in trying to recall the face of my friend Pierre, take from a drawer a photograph of him, a sketch, or a caricature, we can consider concretely the differences between imagining and perceiving. In perception, Sartre explains, the photograph is but a paper rectangle with variously distributed dark and light patches, the sketch and the caricature merely pencil or pen markings on a paper square. These material objects which I perceive can be studied – I can measure the size of the border on the photograph or try to ascertain the finishing process used; I can notice the predominantly vertical slant of the sketch's pencil marks or the alternately thick and thin application of the ink on the caricature. I need never even realize that these dark and light spots, these pen and pencil markings could represent something, someone. But when I do see that they represent Pierre, when I see Pierre in and through them, then, according to Sartre, my consciousness of these objects has become imaginative. I have found a way – through imagination – to make Pierre's face present to me, though Pierre is absent and I know he is absent. *I have put* Pierre into the photograph, sketch, or caricature. These objects do not give him to me; I reach through them to apprehend his face imaginatively.

Sartre's conviction that I do not *perceive* Pierre in the photograph or sketch is a point of fellowship with a large group of philosophers, an extensive community diverse enough to include, for example, both Descartes and Gilbert Ryle.[6] However, Sartre's position becomes rather lonely when he goes on to insist that, not only do I not perceive Pierre in the sketch, but also, when I do reach Pierre imaginatively, I do not perceive the sketch.

> . . . the formation of an imaginative consciousness is accompanied . . . by an annihilation of a perceptual consciousness, and vice versa.
> . . . when one directs attention to Pierre as an image by means of a painting, it means that the painting is no longer perceived
> (*I*, p. 231, and *I(e)*, p. 138).

There are internal features of Sartre's philosophy which lead to this conclusion, but the point can be considered outside of that context. It is true that when a painting is for me a likeness of my friend Pierre, when I am occupied with regarding Pierre's face through the painting, I am unlikely to remark that the paint is nearly half a centimeter thick or that the canvas is primarily brown. When I am using a photograph to bring Pierre's face before me, I may not notice the black spot on the left side of the print, the shadow caused by the clumsy photographer's thumb. Or, to use one of Sartre's examples, if in watching the impersonator Franconay I am suddenly imaginatively aware of Maurice Chevalier, I must no longer perceive Franconay's female body, must no longer see those feminine contours. And the glazed look of those caught in their own daydreams does sometimes lead us to conclude that they do not see what is right before their open eyes.

But despite these sorts of considerations, Sartre's contention seems implausible. He must maintain that when, in a theater, I 'see' (i.e., imagine) Hamlet in the castle, I cannot at the same time be actually seeing Nicol Williamson on the stage. Should I deny that last night I saw Nicol Williamson or say that I have never seen him if, after all, I've only 'seen' his Hamlet? If it takes no effort and no time to become aware of Pierre's face in the photograph, if, upon being presented with the print, I immediately seem to see Pierre, does it follow that I have not seen the photographic print? Sartre is adamant: '. . . to say "I have an image of Pierre" is equivalent to saying not only "I do not see Pierre," but also "I see nothing at all"' (*I*, p. 32, and *I(e)*, p. 13).

While one wonders at Sartre's intransigence, one cannot fail to notice the epistemological advantage he means to secure through his position. If we can perceive and imagine at the same time, if perceiving and imagining are intermingled in our experience, it seems we might need some way of sorting percepts and images. This is Mead's view, and he thinks that the behavior which follows on our experience yields the possibility of such classification: I proceed to embrace the one whom I take to be my friend, but my very approach results in the termination of my intended act; for now I see this is a stranger. Therefore, I dismiss my earlier visual experience as supplied by imagery. Sartre holds, however, that we need neither action nor analysis to disentangle imagery from perception, since these can never be mixed.

But again, Sartre is prepared to defend a still stronger conclusion: not only are images and percepts always separate and distinct from one another, but they are so utterly different in character that this distinction between them is always manifest. In perception, Sartre reminds us, we observe objects; we can continue to learn about them as we change our point of view, can notice features of which we had been unaware. But our attitude toward the object of an image might be called 'quasi-observation'. Having a visual image, we might say that the object is 'seen' from the front. The object is addressed as if from a point of view, but there is no possibility that changing our point of view can reveal anything. We cannot notice new and surprising features in our images; we cannot learn from them. To illustrate with a familiar example, if I am asked to imagine the Pantheon, I may be able to do it. I may have a vivid image of the Pantheon as seen from the front, but if I am then asked to count the columns which support the facade, I cannot do it. I cannot even attempt to count. Either I know the number of columns and can say it without counting, or I

Imagination

cannot say it at all. My image remains clear and distinct, but it is incapable of being studied, of revealing to me what I don't already know. This is what Sartre means when he says that, though 'the object of perception overflows consciousness', 'the image . . . suffers from a sort of essential poverty' (*I*, p. 24, and *I(e)*, p. 8).

Perhaps it is to this 'essential poverty' that Hume wants to allude when he says that ideas, the images of impressions, are distinguished by their relative lack of 'force and liveliness'.[7] But Hume asserts that the only difference between simple impressions and ideas is 'their degree of force and vivacity. . . . When I shut my eyes and think of my chamber, the ideas I form are exact representations of the impressions I felt; nor is there any circumstance of the one, which is not found in the other.'[8]

Hume is among the many who have regarded the mental image as but a faint perception, and it is this view that Sartre is trying to dispel when he describes the phenomenon of quasi-observation. I may have a vivid image of a woman's face and yet be unable to say whether the eyes are dark brown or light blue. If I am perceiving a face, even if I have hitherto not paid attention to the eyes, I can now notice their color. But I cannot study my *image* to learn the color of the imagined eyes. It is not as if the face in my image must, like a real face, have eyes which *are* some particular color, a color waiting, as it were, to be noticed. I can imagine a face without imagining that the eyes are any particular color at all. And if I imagine a small crowd of people, I probably cannot say how many people I am imagining. I certainly cannot count the crowd in my image, as I can count the people in a crowd I see.

Moreover, in Hume's description both impressions and ideas are said to admit of varying degrees of vivacity. Since Hume himself acknowledges that our ideas can be exceedingly forceful and our impressions extremely faint, distinguishing one from the other should often be a difficult task. But in fact we do not usually have to sort through our experience, analyze or compare, in order to determine whether we are having an image of an object or actually perceiving it. This is a point on which Sartre wants to insist. Even a very vivid image does not usually leave one uncertain about its status. It does not teeter on the brink of becoming a perception.

Sartre seems correct in much of his attack on the traditional assimilation of imagining to perceiving. Yet even if one agrees that

Imagination

Sartre has noted and described previously overlooked differences between imagination and perception, and even if one considers this accomplishment important and impressive, one is inclined to think that Sartre's comments fit best the case of the deliberately produced mental image. If I purposely form an image of Pierre's face, the effect *is* utterly distinct and different from actually seeing Pierre's face, no matter how vivid my image, no matter how faint perception can be. And it is true that this fact seems to have been ignored or treated as an embarrassment by accounts which describe the image and the percept as essentially alike.[9] But what of hallucinations and the dreams of sleep? These are usually grouped with exercises of imagination, but they are thought to be imaginings which are *not* immediately recognized as such. Since Sartre maintains that we *cannot* confuse our imagining with perceiving, he obviously faces a difficult task in accounting for dreams and hallucinations. His comments on these phenomena are, in fact, enormously interesting, but a discussion of these topics would lead us too far afield.[10] I mention the cases of the hallucination and the dream only as reminders that, however convincing Sartre's remarks on the characteristic distinctions between having a deliberately produced mental image and perceiving, we must examine separately each function of imagination, each sort of imaginative act.[11]

With a thus renewed respect for the specific case, let us return to the portrait example, recalling Sartre's insistence that when we imaginatively 'see' Pierre through the painting, we cannot at the same time be actually seeing the painting. Has anything been said which should unsettle our rejection of that contention? I think not. The description of quasi-observation reminds us that forming a mental image of Pierre is radically different from actually seeing Pierre in the flesh; it does not show us that 'seeing' Pierre in a portrait is radically different from actually seeing the painting which is this portrait.[12] Seeing the face in the picture does not seem to involve directing attention toward a private image of Pierre; the painting is not simply the occasion for voluntary imagining. Proof of this is found, in Sartre's own terms, in the fact that we can study the Pierre of the portrait. We can notice features we had overlooked ('Look here – see how wrinkled the neck is!'); we can be surprised ('I would never have thought Pierre's face could look so cruel.'); we can learn through our observation

52

Imagination

('So – his eyes *are* blue.'). (A proviso of representational accuracy ('His eyes are blue, provided this painting is faithful.') is here both unnecessary and inappropriate. It is not a question of learning new facts about the Pierre of flesh and blood: I am instead adverting to the difference between our mental images of Pierre – which we cannot study, in which we do not *notice* surprising features – and this painted Pierre – which we can study. I am noting that we seem to be able to *observe* this painted Pierre in a way not very different from the way we can observe the real Pierre. And we must also mark the fact that it is not simply the painting as a physical object that we are thus regarding: We don't say, 'So – there are two patches of blue paint'; we instead discover that he, the painted Pierre, has blue eyes.)

Still, even if we do not turn our attention from the painting when we apprehend Pierre through it, it is possible to perceive the painting without finding Pierre in it. Perhaps it is this circumstance which might tempt one to think that, when Pierre is reached, he is 'seen' in an image and not seen in the painting; since, after all, the painting was seen without its revealing a face and, it must be granted, the canvas hasn't changed. But this analysis should by now have lost its charm. And we can afford to resist its appeal, for a better description is available. We don't switch from seeing only paint on canvas to 'seeing' or having a mental image of Pierre; instead, we move from seeing only the painted canvas to seeing this canvas as a painting of Pierre. We don't cease to see the paint on the canvas; but we now see an aspect of it which we had formerly missed. We may say we see the canvas in a new, a different way, but we don't feel *we've* changed – we feel it is, if anything, the *canvas* which has changed, which *looks* different. Yet we know that the canvas has not changed. We still see those same blue patches of paint, only we now see them as eyes.

Of course, we cannot leave the matter at that. It is notoriously difficult to say what service this particular description is rendering, what it is to 'see . . . as . . . ', and we must at least address the question of what it means that this description is the correct one to use. But I think a path of approach to this awkward question can be prepared, so, partly with that aim, I would like to defer direct consideration of this topic in order to pursue first a somewhat more manageable problem: given that there are obvious and important differences between having a mental image of Pierre

Imagination

and seeing a painting as a picture of Pierre, why does Sartre try to assimilate these cases? Why does he say that seeing Pierre in the painting is 'strictly parallel' to having an image? (*I*, p. 41; *I(e)*, p. 18).

We must note that it is not just paintings which, according to Sartre, can be turned into images. He sets out a wide range of cases which he calls 'the image family'. Photographs, paintings, caricatures, impersonations or imitations, and schematic drawings are part of this family; and it must be these members which have impressed Bernard Williams, for he dismisses Sartre's account by saying: 'Sartre . . . seems to hope that he has acquired enough impetus from the representational cases to convey him through the air to visualization, where our "intention," in his terminology, is not sustained by any matter at all.'[13] It is true that Sartre arranges his examples so that, roughly, less and less representational material is before our eyes – we move through intermediate cases from seeing Pierre in a color snapshot to seeing him in three strokes of ink. This ordering of cases is undoubtedly designed to impart a kind of momentum to Sartre's analysis, but it is certainly not true that Sartre hopes to be propelled 'through the air' to a case where there is no representational material at all. He says that:

> the material of the mental image is more difficult to determine. . . . But . . . it is evident that the mental image must also have a material, and a material which derives its meaning solely from the intention which animates it (*I*, p. 41; *I(e)*, p. 18).

To show how slight the material of the image might be, Sartre reminds us that we can see a cat in the abstract motif of the rug, we can see faces in the fire, and we (some) can even see scenes in a crystal ball.

Sartre includes all these cases in the image family, for he thinks they are all functionally identical: the imaginative consciousness involves making an object 'appear', though the object is not present. This is accomplished by turning some material into a representation of the absent or non-existent object, a task which involves a special use of knowledge. Though he does not himself refrain from using the term 'mental image', Sartre says this expression is misleading; we must understand that the image is not a semblance or a copy, but is, rather, 'a certain way that the object

Imagination

has of appearing to consciousness, or, if one prefers, a certain way that consciousness has of presenting an object to itself' (*I*, p. 20; *I(e)*, 5). The image is a relation, 'un rapport'.

Hide Ishiguro criticizes this analysis by underlining some difficulties Sartre might have with the second term of the claimed relation.[14] She understands that the point of his remarks is to deny that imagining is directing attention on an image: Sartre wants to say that when I have an image of Pierre, the object of my attention is Pierre, the man in Paris, (and not some mental copy of Pierre). But, Ishiguro asks, what is the object of my attention when I picture the goddess Venus? It can't be Venus, in front of Vulcan's forge, for neither she nor such a place exists. It seems there is no appropriate object of attention in the physical world, so it might seem necessary to find a mental object to take the second place in the relation which is the image. But if a mental object is thus required, the promise of the relational analysis is lost. Under these circumstances, Ishiguro thinks it best to abandon completely the explanation of the image as a relation.

Although I do not want to endorse Sartre's relational analysis of the image, it must be remarked that his view is not as flagrantly untenable as Ishiguro's criticisms might suggest. Sartre is not unaware of the fact that we can imagine the non-existent. But he would not take as helpful the suggestion that his theory can account for this fact only by postulating mental objects. His description of the image as a relation was proffered precisely to help dispel belief in mental objects. There may be a confusion in his account, but it is not as obvious or as self-defeating as this.

There is in fact an ambiguity in Sartre's discussion, and I think it is the failure to notice this ambiguity which explains both the particular cast of Ishiguro's criticism and, in addition, the mistaken charge by Bernard Williams mentioned earlier. It happens that Sartre is inconsistent in his isolation of the object of an imaginative consciousness: if I am seeing Pierre in a portrait, Sartre says that I am imaginatively apprehending Pierre, the man, that the Pierre of flesh and blood is the object of my consciousness. But he also says that I am imaginatively apprehending the painting, that the painting, though it is no longer perceived, has become the object of an imaginative consciousness. This inconsistency is engendered, in part, by Sartre's passion to deny the existence of imaginary objects: he says that Pierre, the man, is the object of my

Imagination

consciousness because I am imaginatively aware of *him*, and not perceptually aware of a copy of him. This is one of his ways of emphasizing that:

> There is not a world of images and a world of objects. Every object . . . can function as a present reality or as an image, depending on what center of reference has been chosen. The two worlds, real and imaginary, are composed of the same objects: only the grouping and interpretation of these objects varies (*I*, p. 45; *I(e)*, p. 20).

But, of course, Sartre is well aware that we can have images of the unreal, the non-existent. Again, however, he wants to insist that 'the chimera does not exist "as an image." It exists neither as such nor otherwise' (*I*, p. 20; *I(e)*, p. 5). It doesn't occur to him that this sort of case might be thought a problem for his relational analysis, because he always has available that other object of consciousness, the *material* of the image. In the case of the portrait of Pierre, this material is the painted canvas. My imaginative consciousness is directed on the painting; it can stand in the second place in the relation.

If we take the object of consciousness to be the material of the image and not what the image is of, then the problem Ishiguro sees does not arise. We noted in dismissing Williams' assessment of Sartre's account that Sartre holds that there is *always* some material which functions as an analogue of what's being imagined. The imagining of a chimera is no exception. If I am looking at a painting of such a monster, it is obvious that the material of my imaginative awareness is the colored canvas. But Sartre's artful arrangement of a series of examples should convince us that the material can become extremely meager. I can also see a chimera in a hasty sketch, in a spot of coffee spilled on the white tablecloth, in a shadow, or in the passing clouds. Sartre contends that, as the material becomes more impoverished, knowledge plays an increasingly important role.

He says that we interpret the material and 'fill in its gaps' (*I*, p. 104; *I(e)*, p. 57) in *any* imaginative act, but the gaps to be filled vary with each case. The painting can nearly seem to present Pierre's face; it can be almost as if I find it there. But I do not feel I discover Pierre's face in the cloud; I put it there – I construct it out of that amorphous matter. If we remember that Sartre's examples

Imagination

can well be described as instances of seeing one thing as another ('I see these pencil lines as a chimera', 'I see that coffee stain as a face'), then we might recall Wittgenstein's remark that 'the flashing of an aspect on us seems half visual experience, half thought' (*PI*, p. 197).

The visualization of a chimera, in contrast to the seeing of one in a coffee stain, may still seem to pose a problem of analysis. But we should now admit that this case is no more troublesome than the visualization of Pierre. For Sartre, the problem is the isolation of the *material* of the image. The existent Pierre is not the *material* of my image of him, so it doesn't matter that the chimera doesn't exist. What Sartre thinks must exist in these cases of visualization, as in all imaginative acts, is some material which can serve as a representative, an analogue – something which an imaginative consciousness can apprehend as the non-existent chimera or the absent Pierre. Sartre feels he is reduced to conjecture on this topic, that he must leave what he calls 'the sure ground of phenomenological description' (*I*, p. 111; *I(e)*, p. 62). He thinks we may draw on various intrasomatic elements when we form mental images – entoptic lights, myogenic and kinaesthetic sensations are among the possibilities he suggests. These proposals are not wholly implausible. If I can see Pierre in a cloud, why not in a phosphene?

I do not, however, want to examine Sartre's attempt to sustain these conjectures. I think it would be appropriate, instead, to redirect attention on the controversy which occasioned this discussion, because I think certain conclusions are waiting to be drawn.

ACCOMMODATION WITHIN ANOTHER VIEW

Mead said that our perceptions are often mixed with, filled out by our imaginings. His plea for this claim did not seem persuasive. But Sartre's conviction that perceiving and imagining are always utterly and obviously distinct was also rejected. Nonetheless, in locating our dissatisfactions with Sartre's position, we found that many of his intuitions could not be dismissed. And it seems to me that the path of their accommodation takes us, in addition, to an understanding of what is right about Mead's assertions.

Imagination

We realized that we could employ the 'see . . . as . . .' formula to describe some of Sartre's examples ('I see those blue patches of paint as eyes'), but we haven't remarked that it fits examples of the sort Mead proposes as well. ('From that distance, in the dusk, I took the highway sign to be a hitchhiker. I saw the sign posts as legs, the left section of the sign as the head and body, and the right section as a backpack.') Sartre insists that these cases, ones where we, but not Sartre, find it appropriate to use the 'see . . . as . . .' expression, should be grouped not under the heading 'perception', but under 'imagination'. Mead, on the other hand, while ultimately regarding these as cases of imagining, emphasizes their connection, their continuity, with perceiving. I think there is some justification for each's attitude. Wittgenstein says of 'seeing . . . as . . .' that 'it is like seeing and again not like' (*PI*, II, p. 197).

In order to help motivate Sartre's position, let us first examine one way in which 'seeing . . . as . . .' is not like seeing. We can use as a foil a claim by Hide Ishiguro. In arguing against Sartre's view that an imaginative consciousness requires the annihilation of a perceptual one, Ishiguro says that '[o]ne cannot see X as Y without seeing X.'[15] But this claim seems to me to reflect a mistake, and I think that if we are ever to elucidate 'seeing . . . as . . .', the mistake must be made plain. Let us consider a professional conjuror's trick – for instance, the Headless Woman illusion mentioned by J. L. Austin. A woman is on a black stage with a black bag over her head. We are to see this hooded woman as a headless woman. Ishiguro says we cannot see X as Y without seeing X, but if we see on the stage a woman with a bag on her head, we have failed to see a headless woman – we must *not* see the hooded head. One could cast about for a different substitution for X – one might say, for example, that we see the *apparition* as a headless woman – but this defense is trivializing. Of course *something* must be there to be seen as Y; and this 'something' can be described or referred to in many different ways. But, as Ryle has pointed out, 'see' is an achievement word. So when I see an X as a Y, even though I am looking at an X, even though X must be there in order for me to see X as a Y, I need not be, need not succeed in, seeing X. Moreover, in this particular example, we must admit that we do not really see Y either: we see a hooded woman as a headless woman, but there is, after all, no headless woman to be seen.

Imagination

That might, then, be some justification for Sartre's attitude, for the account of these cases he prefers. But Mead's approach is also warranted. Let us compare Wittgenstein's example:

> I am shewn a picture-rabbit and asked what it is; I say 'It's a rabbit.' Not 'Now it's a rabbit.' I am reporting my perception. – I am shewn the duck-rabbit and asked what it is; I *may* say 'It's a duck-rabbit.' . . . – The answer that it is a duck-rabbit is again the report of a perception; the answer 'Now it's a rabbit' is not. Had I replied 'It's a rabbit,' the ambiguity would have escaped me, and I should have been reporting my perception (*PI*, II, p. 195).

Against this set the problem of the highway sign mistaken for a hitchhiker. I say that I saw the posts as legs and the various sections of the billboard as the head, body, and backpack. Mead would call this a case of imagining, but he would want to emphasize its connection with perceiving. So, as he would characterize it, when I see the object in the dusky distance and I say, 'There's a hitchhiker', I am reporting a *perception*. Later, when I realize that that perception was idiosyncratic, I reclassify it as imaginary. But this means that I have now recognized the ambiguity in the situation. Only *now* can I say of my earlier visual experience 'I saw the sign posts as legs.' Earlier, when there was for me no ambiguity, the correct report of my perception was 'there is [or 'I see'] a hitchhiker.' ('I see the backpack', etc.)

Thus, Mead is tempted to characterize his examples as cases where we *perceive* imagery. But if we admit that a better description is in terms of 'seeing . . . as . . .', we can begin to understand the motivation for some of Mead's other remarks, the remarks we earlier found internally inconsistent. Mead said, we remember, that what distinguishes imagery is its appearance in the absence of the object to which it refers. Now notice that there is a limitation on the use of the 'see . . . as . . .' formula which corresponds to that intuition: we cannot, as a general rule, see Y as Y.[16] Wittgenstein says that one cannot say at the sight of a knife and fork that one is seeing them *as* a knife and fork: 'One doesn't "*take*" what one knows as the cutlery at a meal *for* cutlery' (*PI*, II, p. 195).

But one knows these objects to be cutlery because one has had a certain upbringing, because one lives in a certain social setting.

And there are different ways in which one's background might block the possibility of 'seeing . . . as . . .' *I* can't see the knife and fork *as* tools for eating because, to me, that is simply what they *are*. But one who has lived all of his or her life using rolled palm leaves to convey food from bowl to mouth may *fail* to see a knife and fork as dining implements. Neither of us sees these objects as tools for eating, and, in each case, we can't see them *as* this because of our social settings – but the different social settings obstruct 'seeing . . . as . . .' in different ways. Another sort of case would be my inability to see Pierre as the very image of his father, when I haven't ever seen his father. I do in general notice resemblances between people, I *can* pick out such similarities; but I here lack a particular requisite experience.

It is the connection between background experience and capability that Mead can perhaps be stressing when he says that '[an image] could always be referred to the experiences out of which [it arose].' If we want an explanation for our seeing X as Y, one field which must be searched is our background. We can find in our own histories, in our past experiences, our education, our social context *reasons* not only for our ability to see this X as Y, but also for our inability to see it so – reasons even for the fact that we are now, at this moment of our lives, seeing, or not seeing, it so.[17]

There is no reason why Mead should not welcome dismissal of the talk of 'perceiving imagery' in favor of employment of the 'seeing . . . as . . .' formula.[18] In fact, his particular version of behaviorism and pragmatism could well constitute a standpoint from which the latter sort of characterization would naturally arise. Seeing a face in the clouds is an exercise of the imagination, but if we say that this is a matter of seeing the cloud *as* a face, we are less inclined to feel that the mystery of this imaginative act will be resolved by postulation of a mental object. And if we don't postulate a mental object of attention, then the important features of the situation are not inherently closed to public examination and understanding. There is no crucial element, the private mental image, which *cannot* be revealed or discovered. If I am seeing the cloud as a face, and you want to understand that situation, the elements you must study are the cloud and me (including, for example, my past experiences). Understanding the situation may be a relatively complicated matter, and the paths of access to its various elements may be exceedingly tortuous, but it's not as if attempts at approach are inevitably misguided. There is not necessarily an element which is always and absolutely beyond public reach. And to see how open not just the element, but even the fact of the situation's occurrence can be, we might consider the case where one is suddenly struck by a likeness: one suddenly sees Pierre as the image of his father. Wittgenstein remarks: 'If someone who knew me had seen my face he would have said "Something about his face struck you just now"' (*PI*, II, p. 211).

The way I have seen something will often be disclosed by my reactions and by my observable attitudes. The concept of 'seeing . . . as . . .' is closely related to 'regarding . . . as . . .' and 'treating . . . as . . .' And just as the way I treat something (someone, some situation) can depend on my purposes, my purposes can affect the way I see something (someone, some situation). So, to understand my seeing X as Y we might have to study my interests and goals, in addition to my past experiences and present context. But the connection between 'seeing . . . as . . .' and 'treating . . . as . . .' suggests that the phenomenon of seeing X as Y is accessible through yet another channel: the fact that I have seen X as Y may be immediately expressed in *action*.

Hence, the feature of life so emphasized by Mead and the other pragmatists, action, *is* a part of this phenomenon, and the terms of analysis acceptable to Mead do not seem inappropriate or obviously inadequate. But even if Mead might find it worthwhile to investigate 'seeing . . . as . . .', and even if he could happily assimilate some of the occurrences he calls 'imaginings' to cases of seeing X as Y, we might feel that some of the most ordinary examples of imagining clearly resist accommodation in this framework. If I, alone in my room – bereft of photographs, sketches, coffee stains, and clouds – *visualize* Pierre, it surely doesn't seem there is any *object* I am seeing *as* Pierre. And if the concept of 'seeing . . . as . . .' cannot help us to understand this sort of case, might we not, after all, need recourse from the world of real objects to a world of images?

Mead, in considering that the sight of a room might recall to one an individual whom one has met there, offers something like a neurological account of the image. But he goes on to say:

What is still unexplained in such a statement of association is the fact that one image appears rather than the countless others which have also been a part of the experience of the room. The customary explanation derived from frequency and vividness . . . proves inadequate, and we must fall back upon impulses seeking expression . . . upon interest, upon attention. The so-called 'selective nature' of consciousness is as necessary for the explanation of association as for that of attention and shows itself in our sensitivity to the stimuli which set free impulses seeking expression . . . (*MSS*, p. 341).

Sartre says that the image is presented as a kind of absence, a 'nothingness'. But he also says that we apprehend nothingness on the foundation of the real, the existent world. If I, searching for Pierre, enter a room full of people, if all my hopes and expectations are focused on Pierre, the others in the room may be, only a background, a context. And if Pierre is not there, I pay no heed to the presence of Mary, John, and the others. I see only the absence of Pierre. I see the room as a place lacking Pierre.

We might remember Hume's fear that the perception of 'a blank' proves an exception to his empiricist maxim. He asserts that, if a spectrum missing one shade of blue were to be placed before a normally sighted adult, that individual would *perceive a gap* and, what's more, would be able to fill the gap with an image underived from a sense impression.

But we don't need to share Hume's worry about or assessment of this case; and we don't need to claim images are not in some way based on past experience when we admit that I could see my empty room as a place without Pierre. I have, as Mead puts it, 'an impulse seeking expression', 'an interest', and this interest is in *seeing* Pierre's face. So I visualize it. We needn't say that I am seeing a mental image. Rather, the sight of my room as a place without Pierre to be seen involves here the thought of Pierre's appearance. It is thus that Pierre may come to me, appear to me, in thought, in his absence.

SEEING . . . AS . . . AND CONTEXTS OF INTERPRETATION

If we have, then, found a new way to think about the problematic

Imagination

issue of visualization, if we have found a way of talking about visualization in terms of 'seeing . . . as . . .', still, we should not want to insist that there are not differences to be marked between the cases of, say, seeing those paint daubs as eyes and visualizing Pierre.

Even between examples which seem more closely related – seeing the paint daubs as eyes and seeing the sign posts as legs – we might note important differences. These two examples are alike in their involvement of actual objects of sight, in there being rather particular material things one must actually be looking at. But the example of the highway sign differs from that of the paint daubs in the necessity we feel to establish the sign as, or to explain its being, an object seen as something other than itself. With the paint daubs, or, surely, with some inkblots, the name of the game can *be* 'interpretation'. But with the highway sign we must establish a context of interpretation by first announcing our departure from ordinary perception: 'I took it to be a . . .', 'I thought it was a . . .', 'I mistook it for a . . .'[19] And it seems only after the stage has thus been set, the fact of interpretation introduced, that the locution of imaginative apprehension or projection can make a comfortable entrance. After you know I mistook one whole object for another, I can easily fasten my mistake on particular features of that object: 'I saw *this* as a . . .', '. . . *that* as a . . .'

It is true that we may not need to establish ourselves within a theater of interpretation in order to say of whole objects 'I see it as . . .' That locution could be the immediate resort for those familiar with the two aspects of the duck-rabbit drawing, with the two readings of a reversible figure/ground picture, for those playing idle or probing games with inkblots, doodles, or clouds. But it is in these cases antecedently clear that interpretation – some interpretation or another – must be in play. We would not say of a portrait of Pierre rendered in standard Renaissance fashion that we see it – the painting or the canvas or the paint – *as* Pierre. But then, *pace* Sartre, neither would we say that seeing the Pierre in or of this portrait requires an exercise of imagination.

When we say of a flesh and blood human being that we see him or her as X we cannot, then, be announcing a mistaken sense perception; we must be offering an interpretation, an interpretation acknowledged as such in that very choice of words. Thus, if we want to capture the point of the case which intrigued Mead, the case of the individual first seen from a distance and now approached, we do not say: 'I saw him as my friend'; we proclaim our mistake, our mistaking of the whole sight, with, e.g.: 'I thought it was my friend.' (And we can, perhaps, explain: 'I saw that fellow's high collar as Pierre's beard, his hair as that cap Pierre wears', etc.) The words 'I saw [or, "see"] him as my friend' are likely to be embedded in another context altogether, to be uttered in a discussion which is grounded in the necessity of interpretation. (The past tense version might indeed suggest the rueful description of a mistake, but, of course, the mistake would not have been one connected with, attributable to, one of the five senses, to a false, idiosyncratic, or 'imaginary' sense perception.)

The fact that the 'see . . . as . . .' locution does not provide a summary statement of Mead's favored example, is not used to describe a mistaken or errant perception (wandering from the world to me as it is reclassified as imaginary), is not an unwelcome discovery. For what is revealed is that in the application of that locution to human beings – to, as it were, 'whole' human beings, as opposed to features of them – their collars, their hair, etc. – that locution always suggests not a mistake but an interpretation, and the necessity of interpretation. And we have seen that this sort of interpretation can involve something which is not inappropriately called 'imagination'.

If a reminder is needed, Strawson warns that:

> The uses, and applications of the terms 'image,' 'imagine,' 'imagination,' 'imaginative,' and so forth make up a very diverse and scattered family. Even this image of a family seems too definite. It would be a matter of more than difficulty exactly to identify and list the family members, let alone establish their relationships of parenthood and cousinhood.[20]

I have not tried to trace a full genealogy of this family or to set down descriptions of everything which might be called 'an image', 'imagining', or 'imagination'. Nor have I proposed a complete account or explanation of 'seeing . . . as . . .'.

Instead, I have attended to a particular consanguinity. The concepts of 'seeing . . . as . . .' and 'imagining' and even 'having an image' seem, at some points, not merely connected but cognate. I have tried to sketch portions of the shape of these concepts to show not just a similarity but a congruence. An outline

Imagination

thus emerges of an idea of imagination not incompatible with the general cast of Mead's thought.

To develop this idea of imagination, and to see if it can be usefully employed in the theoretical structure which houses Mead's remarks about the self, we must return to those remarks, return to Mead's discussion of the self.

3
THE SELF AS AN OBJECT OF IMAGINATION

THE SELF AND THE CORPOREAL

Although Mead's analysis isolates the vocal gesture as the central factor in the generation and possession of the self, there are moments when he is impressed by a different picture. He thinks of situations of intense, physically absorbing action and is reminded of 'a contrast between an experience that is absolutely wound up in outside activity in which the self as an object does not enter, and an activity of memory and imagination in which the self is the principal object' (*MSS*, p. 137). I would like to begin to develop this picture. What does it mean for the self to be an object of imagination?

In the *Second Meditation*, after Descartes finds the 'unshakably certain element' which not even the most radical skeptical supposition can uproot, he examines the nature of 'this "I" that necessarily exists.' His conclusion is that he is a thinking thing and that the mind is better known than the body, but he finds his own mind wandering, bridling under the restraint of proper, truthful self-aquaintance:

> . . . it still appears, and I cannot help thinking, that corporeal objects, whose images are formed in consciousness, and which the senses actually examine, are known much more clearly than this 'I', this 'something I know not what', which does not fall

The self as an object of imagination

under imagination. It is indeed surprising that I should comprehend more distinctly things that I can tell are doubtful, unknown, foreign to me, than what is real, what I am aware of – my very self.[1]

Descartes says the 'I' 'does not fall under imagination' because 'imagination consists in contemplating the likeness of a body.'[2] And because Descartes takes himself to have shown, through metaphysical doubt, the distinction between this 'I' and anything 'of the nature of body', he must conclude that 'nothing I can comprehend by the help of imagination belongs to my conception of myself.' Still, and seemingly inexplicably, his mind troubles him as it persists in wandering to the corporeal.

Now Mead does not even pretend to doubt away the body, but he does, all the same, distinguish it from the self. His discrimination follows his understanding of reflexivity as the feature which characterizes the self. The body, he says, cannot experience itself as a whole. The eye can see the foot and the left hand can feel the right, but we cannot see our own backs and our left hands cannot feel our own left wrists. So we make a distinction between the biological individual and the self, and we say that the parts of the body 'belong to the self' (*MSS*, p. 136).

Although the notion of reflexivity is central to Mead's conception of the self, his remarks on that notion are brief. I will want to say that reflexivity is achieved in an act of imagination in which one sees oneself as (something or other). To begin to explain this claim and to join the issue of the distinction between the self and the body, I want to consider a passage from Wittgenstein's *Investigations* and prepare for the question '*What* is it one sees in seeing oneself as (X)?'

> I say of someone else 'He seems to believe . . .' and other people say it of me. Now, why do I never say it of myself, not even when others *rightly* say it of me? – Do I myself not see and hear myself, then? – That can be said (*PI*, II, p. 191).

The proscription of 'I seem to believe . . .' may be somewhat hasty. (Imagine a scene of exasperated reflection on and summation of the characteristic history of a particular personal relationship: 'What a fool I am! You come to me with the most preposterous excuses and I accept them! I seem to believe everything you say . . .!') But there are circumstances in which, though others would rightly say of me, 'She seems to believe . . .', I could not say it of myself. Nonetheless, there might be available first-person equivalents or counterparts: 'She seems to believe his side of the story.' 'It looks as if I believe his side of the story, (but I really have no feelings about that quarrel at all; I just don't want to hear any more about it. . . .'); or, 'It must look as if I believe his side of the story, (because my encounters with her have been so tense these past few days. But there's an entirely different reason for that tension.') And, in other cases: 'If it sounds as if I believe that that kind of aggressiveness should be rewarded, then I have not made my position clear . . .'; or, 'It sounds as if I believe my sister has been sabotaging me. Could that really be what I think? It is true that I have sometimes found myself fearing and resenting her friendly advice.'

The fact that we turn to these verbs linked with perception ('It *sounds* . . ., It *looks* as if I believe . . .') to produce the first-person correlates suggests a knowledge of what produces the third-person attributions. Others hear what we say, see what we do, and they draw their conclusions ('She seems to believe . . .') directly. Or, perhaps, they see us directly, hear us directly, and their attributions follow that direct perception. We match their statements indirectly, by taking a position outside ourselves from which we see ourselves, hear ourselves, reach or acknowledge the plausibility of conclusions based on our behavior.

Of course our assertions that we believe are not ordinarily based on observation at all. These cases are special because they are not (just) assertions of belief but are, one way or another, instances of reflection on belief. Of course ordinarily 'one does not infer one's own conviction from one's words' (*PI*, II, p. 191), but one can derive a picture of conviction from one's words. And in those moments of derivation a certain division is marked: either one contrasts the picture of belief with one's real belief, or, as in the last example, one admits that the picture of belief may be accurate after all and that one might, by accepting it, leave a state of confusion or ignorance. Reflection is thus achieved in these cases by attending to one's words and deeds, to the words and deeds there to be perceived by others.

But one's attending is not identical with the perceiving of the

The self as an object of imagination

others. My statement that 'It sounds as if I believe . . .' is not based on hearing my own words any more than my knowledge that my actions must look, for example, partial to him, requires that I see my interactions with her in a mirror. I am, nonetheless, focusing on my words and actions. I am attending to things which are, in a broad Cartesian sense, corporeal – words actually uttered and deeds actually done. And these things are dependent on, part of, my corporeal existence. But my encounter with these elements of the corporeal is not, in these moments of reflection, anchored in one of the five senses.

A similar set of complexities can be discerned in some of the occasions on which an individual might say 'I see myself as (X).' A man reflecting on his role at his family's overwrought reunions says, 'I see myself as the peace-maker.' He might be thinking of his attempts to keep A and B off the subject of politics, his burial of the old can of worms C and D were about to open, his intervention between E and F as they clashed in setting a site for next year's reunion. He might actually picture these specific events, remembering A and B's volatile conversation and the distractions he interjected to dampen their ardor. He muses about his own and his family's conduct, recalling their behavior, perhaps their words, their tones, their physical attitudes. But as he sees himself as a peacemaker he does something more or other than merely to focus on A's words to B, B's words to A, his words to them both, where and how they were all standing, etc. His object of attention is, as was noted initially, a role, the role which he takes his behavior to illustrate and fulfill. He sees a connection between what he said and did here and what he said and did there and between all those actions and whatever actions could truly be called 'peacemaking'. This is an interpretation of his conduct.

Now, although it is his deeds done and his words spoken which ground the man's interpretation of himself, he did not, of course, see or hear those deeds and words, or, did not perceive them just as the others did. Nonetheless, he tries to seize something like a perception of his own actions. Even in this example, where he characterizes himself as a certain sort of agent, he is trying for an objective grasp of his agency. He must have a sense of his actions which goes beyond agency, a sense of his actions as public behavior, behavior which *looks* like and which *sounds* like, in this case, peacemaking. He must objectify his actions because, to make the comparisons and connections of his interpretation, he needs *objects* of comparison.

We find here, then, the reflexivity characteristic of the self. And what is the object of reflection? In this example it is, to repeat, something grounded on actual behavior; and this behavior is, again in a broad and loose Cartesian sense, 'corporeal'. It is, after all, something that 'the senses [of others] actually examine.' In other cases ('I see myself as presidential material') it could be what we might call 'potential behavior'. In yet other cases ('I see myself as fairly resilient') it could be some combination of the actual and the potential. A person may well want to draw a distinction between his or her public behavior and some secret inner core; but the idea of a core completely divorced from any and all behavior, a core which never does and never would in any circumstances find expression, a core which never does and never would cast even a shadow on the public husk, does not seem compelling. (Consider, for example, the boisterous, animated, gregarious woman who insists, 'I see myself as a shy person.' She might indeed be covering her social discomfort with a public disguise. But then she knows what her behavior would be if she for once gave up the effort and dropped her act of concealment. Moreover, her strenuous compensation might be evident to some as just that – her gaiety might be labored enough to be obvious as the defensive behavior of a basically shy person. Or there is the third possibility that she is simply wrong in her judgment of herself: either she doesn't know what it really is to be shy, and so she misconceives her social problems and mistakenly labels herself with a term whose meaning is quite foreign to her, a term no one else could think appropriate; or, she has nothing in mind at all when she makes this aberrant self-description. She may have, however, a motive which fills this vacuum; perhaps, for example, she associates shyness with femininity.) But however essential the corporeal elements may be to reflection, one moves beyond, if through them in the imaginative act of interpretation.

When Wittgenstein introduces the topics of interpretation and 'seeing as' in section xi of Part II of the *Investigations*, he notes two uses of the word 'see': one in which, in response to 'What do you see there?' I say 'I see *this*' and produce a description or a copy, and one in which I say 'I see a likeness between these two.' 'The

The self as an object of imagination

importance of this is', he says, 'the difference of category between the two "objects" of sight' (*PI*, II, p. 193). Suppose the man at the family reunion is able to see [a reflected image of] all his own actions: his sister is a ballet teacher, and they are holding the party in her mirror-lined studio. Now he can see himself laughing and moving between A and B; and he can see himself as a peacemaker; and we can see an important difference of category between the 'objects' of sight.

There is a tension in Mead's thought as he stresses that the body is not the self (*MSS*, p. 136), that the physiological organism must be distinguished from the self (*MSS*, p. 139, p. 187), and he allows that the body can become a self (*MSS*, p. 50), that the physical organism can become an object to itself, the self (*MSS*, p. 137). Mead depends on the idea of emergence to afford a resolution of this tension, but his straits with the distinction between the self and the body are not wholly smoothed by the tide of evolution.[3] He does not want to regard his separation of body and self as fixed, final, metaphysically real. He prefers to emphasize the utility of the distinction to mark different levels of organizational analysis. Although he admits that some people – people who believe in ghosts and 'doubles', for example, believe that the self is actually an entity separable from the body, he is not himself inclined to this belief. (Cf. *MSS*, p. 140.)

When William James discusses the possibility of there being any number of equally true conceptions of the world and its parts, he suggests that each of these conceptions involves 'an addition to some sensible reality'.[4] The illustrations he offers to support this suggestion are described as cases of 'treating . . . as . . .', 'taking . . . as . . .' – 'You can take a chess board as black squares on a white ground, or as white squares on a black ground . . .' – and some of them could well be described in terms of 'seeing . . . as . . .' [Cf., especially, the figure [✡], which can be seen 'as a star, as two big triangles crossing each other, as a hexagon with legs set up on its angles, as six equal triangles hanging together by their tips, etc.' (James, *Pragmatism*, p. 121).] Now even if Mead were to accept the claim that the reflexivity of selfhood is achieved when one sees oneself as (X), he would be uneasy with the simplicity of the Jamesian suggestion that this achievement is worked by some 'addition' to reality. But neither is he comfortable with the alternative, with the idea that the attainment of self-consciousness does not constitute ontological augmentation; because, and this was his starting point, he thinks bodies are incapable of the total reflexivity which is the essential characteristic of the self.

He says that the body cannot experience itself as a whole. One wants a clearer specification of this incapacity. If the left hand cannot feel the left wrist, still, the eye can see that wrist. And if the eye cannot see itself, still, the hand can touch the eye. If we do not insist upon laying open to sight and touch all our internal structures – if we do not, that is, treat our bodies as corpses appropriate for dissection and invasive inspection – isn't it possible for the body to experience all of itself? It can experience itself, Mead says, but not as a whole: these kinds of experiences of portions of the body remain fragmentary; they have to be organized about, related to, the self. They belong, as do the body parts, to the self. Thus Mead's denial of, or dissatisfaction with, the body's reflexivity verges on a denial of the body's integrity. Mead himself does often seem to think of the body not as a whole, but as a collection of parts. He then finds these parts not sufficient to constitute the self, and he seems too, sometimes, to doubt their necessity. The grisly spectre of amputation, which so commonly haunts discussions of personal identity, makes its appearance as Mead declares that '[w]e can lose parts of the body without any serious invasion of the self' (*MSS*, p. 136). We might wonder whether it is this anatomical approach to the body, the analysis by dissection, which is itself the fatal barrier to any coherent presentation of the body as capable of reflexivity.

TOTAL REFLEXIVITY

Whatever our diagnosis of the problem of the reflexivity of the body, and whether or not we think the body capable of total reflexivity, we must be struck by the sudden diminution, the weakening, of the requirement of totality when Mead discusses the vocal gesture. If Mead finds himself dissatisfied with the sort of partial reflexivity which even he grants the body, how can he think that the vocal gesture produces an experience which answers his demands? As I have already argued: even if we were to yield to

The self as an object of imagination

Mead's claim that we hear our utterances just as those around us do, we would not accede to the idea that an individual hearing his own vocal gesture is thereby apprehending himself as a whole. Even if the vocal gesture heard by its maker just as it is heard by others is an object to its maker, that object cannot comprise the whole of the self. Our utterances are certainly expressions of ourselves, but can any particular speech present the experience of the whole self or the self as a whole?

A particular utterance might, of course, be characteristic. But a judgment, a sense, that it is entails an antecedent or supplemental sense of the character which it typifies. However, playing on the histrionic use of these words, we might note that a character can be fully presented in his or her role; the role defines the character. If we remember that some cases of seeing oneself as (X) involve focusing one's attention on a role, we would have reason to think that we have indeed isolated a mode of total reflexivity, that we have found an experience that succeeds, where the vocal gesture fails, in presenting the self as a whole. The man who sees himself as a peacemaker goes beyond awareness of his discrete particular acts to a unified conception of those acts; he grasps them as belonging to a whole, to this role of peacemaking.

There remains, of course, a distinction between experiencing the self as a whole and experiencing the whole of the self. And if we contend that an individual experiences the self as a whole in seeing himself or herself as (X), we do not suppose that this is an experience of the whole self. It is not merely that we might want to allow the passage of time a place in the structure of the self, so that we would not have to claim a whole new self at each moment when a new self-interpretation is available. (The man who sees himself as a peacemaker at today's family reunion may have yesterday, at a business luncheon, seen himself as a cunning fox.) Even at the same moment of time, an individual might extract for attention a variety of roles. (He sees himself as a peacemaker, as a dutiful son, as a devoted husband, as a cunning fox.) Even at one brief moment and even thinking of or drawing upon the same behavior, one could see oneself in a variety of ways, in genuinely different but not necessarily incompatible ways. (He sees himself as a peacemaker, as passionless, as a preserver of the past, as nobody's favorite.) There need be no feeling of closure. One interpretation need not exhaust the object. In fact, as we have noted previously, the very use of the 'see . . . as . . .' expression is suggestive of alternative possibilities.

If this act of imagination does not, then, necessarily involve production of a whole self, if the self as a whole object is not grasped in entirety, must we conclude that imagination fails as a mechanism of reflection, that it is inadequate for the task of total reflexivity required of the self? We would consider this conclusion only if we were assured that the reflection of selfhood does require a full, a complete, a whole object. Mead seems to want to give this assurance, to persevere himself in this conviction even though his own theory's instrument of reflection, the vocal gesture, breaks down well before such a unified object is sighted. He says that 'the total individual organism' (*MSS*, p. 172) must become an object to itself, and this object, this self, must be 'organized' (*MSS*, p. 162), organized into a 'unity' (*MSS*, p. 160), a 'whole self' (*MSS*, p. 152). If, however, we could not find sufficient motivation to sustain this notion of the self as a unified object, we certainly would not think a unified whole should be the target of reflection. Then, far from showing the inaptness of imagination for the essential capacity of selfhood, the fact that an act of imaginative interpretation does not yield a whole self would be a point of merit.

To begin to assess our intuitions on this issue we would do well to explore the theory of unification proposed by Mead in his remarks on play and games. Such an exploration would not only deepen our sense of the differences between Mead's account of the self and one which would place imagination at the heart of self-consciousness; it would also probe the range of accord between the latter sort of account and the broader theoretical guidelines staked out by Mead.

I have already tried to suggest that his commitment to behaviorism and pragmatism need not involve a dismissal of imagination as beyond the ken, as off the paths of understanding which he would tread. I have also tried to show something of the way in which a particular sort of imaginative act – seeing oneself as (X) – realizes the achievement of self-consciousness: we have seen that some of the terms in which Mead discusses the power of the vocal gesture are applicable to the imaginative act; there is in it something like an identification with or an attempt at indirect

The self as an object of imagination

access to, the perceptions of others. Thus Mead's description of the attainment of the self fits this exercise of imagination. But that description was, for Mead, schematic, the inchoate indication of the structural requirements he develops in his remarks on play and games. We should return, then, to those remarks in order to assess his detailed picture of the unified self. As we proceed with that assessment, however, we want to keep a firm hold on the materials of comparison that we now carry with us. We have seen that the alternative conception ties the self to imagination, and suggests that the accomplishment of reflexivity is evident in the acts in which an individual sees himself as (X). This conception needs and will receive further development, but it might be well at this point to take a few bearings on the course of that development. For that purpose, I need to repeat and augment an important disclaimer.

The prominence of 'seeing . . . as . . .' in the discussion thus far has not stemmed from a belief that seeing . . . as . . . is involved in all acts of imagination or is at the core of an act which is central to or can provide the key to all aspects of imagination, imagining, images. It is true that I have tried to trace the congruence of seeing . . . as . . . and visualizing and that I have tried to display the bonds between visualizing and acts of imagination which do incorporate seeing and actual objects of sight; and visualizing has often provoked disproportionate interest from philosophers – as if it were the whole or the core or the most interesting or troublesome sort of imagining.

So, of course, has vision been the prime mode of perception for the epistemologists, perhaps for some good reasons; it is often treated as the dominant, the most important sense. (Its epistemological centrality even seems enshrined in the language, as 'to see' can also mean to understand ('I see your point'), to discover or learn ('See what they want'), and to make certain ('See that the job is done correctly').) And, as attention to the other sense is slighted, comments and conclusions about vision are thought either to cover the field of perception or to need only a few inconsequential additions to do so. This attitude is undoubtedly a source of distortion and error.

Nevertheless, my own excuse for emphasizing seeing . . . as . . . is, in fact, that I have wanted to draw out and rely upon its connection with that commonly discussed sense, vision. One virtue of this connection is that it easily brings to the force the sensuous elements of imaginative reflection and so underscores the relation between the self and the body, the corporeal.

Furthermore, a mode of imagination linked conceptually with the most thoroughly perspectival sense can be most easily tied to the achievement of gaining a perspective on oneself and sharing the viewpoints of others. The word 'perspective' is etymologically allied to sight, and the notion itself either cannot be developed with reference to the other senses or allows a development which is comparatively attenuated. (The contact senses of touch and taste allow no relevant sense of perspective, and neither, really, does smell. One can follow one's nose to the source of a smell, but one isn't thus obtaining different olfactory perspectives. One either smells it or one doesn't, and the difference in the sense experience when one is here and when one is there is only a difference of degree, a difference in the strength of the smell. Hearing seems the only genuine contender as a perspectival sense. One's distance from and position in relation to, for example, a symphony orchestra make a difference, an important and a qualitative difference, in the nature of one's perception. Nonetheless, the differences of auditory perspective are probably much less noticed and far less important than those of visual perspective in the everyday lives of most people, (record producers and acoustic engineers perhaps aside): we all often move to get a good or a better look at something, but we don't speak of trying for a better 'hear' or 'listen'.)

I shall depend upon that strong link between a mode of imagination and the gaining of new and different perspectives as I later try to build a fuller account of the relation between the self and aspects of imagination not so significantly tied to sense perception. For now, however, I note that a particular visual perspective does not at once disclose every bit of an object which it might discover, and I note again that the imaginative sight of the self as an object does not reveal the whole of the self. With our attention thus refocused on the worries about unification of the self, we turn again to Mead's theory.

The self as an object of imagination

PLAY AND GAME

A brief recapitulation is in order: Mead discusses play and game as illustrative of the processes integral to the exercise of self-consciousness and as activities in which a child must engage in order to develop and possess a self. In play the child takes different roles, plays at being mother, teacher, policeman. He responds as mother might to situations, to stimuli, he himself presents. This is, Mead says, the simplest form of being another to one's self. The complications of the game are experienced in a second stage of self-development. The game requires of the child not just the capacity to assume a variety of roles; he or she must also understand the relationships which obtain among the roles. The game is organized as the role-taking of play is not, and the child's responses in the game must be appropriate to, controlled by that organization. His or her position is defined by, his or her actions governed by, a structure which encompasses the positions, the actions, the expectations of the other participants. This structure, this organization of the attitudes of all the participants constitutes a different sort of 'other' – not a particular other: not a parent, teacher, friend – but a 'generalized other'. The realization of the generalized other engenders the unity, the wholeness of the self. It is Mead's judgment that

> in play . . . there is just a set of responses that follow on each other indefinitely. At such a stage we speak of a child as not yet having a fully developed self. . . . He does not organize his life as we would like to have him do, namely as a whole. . . . The child reacts to a certain stimulus, and the reaction is in himself that is called out in others, but he is not a whole self. In his game he has to have an organization of these roles. . . . The game represents the passage in the life of the child . . . to the [organization] . . . that is essential to self-consciousness in the full sense of the term (*MSS*, p. 152).

If the given human individual is to develop a self in the fullest sense, it is not sufficient for him merely to take the attitudes of other human individuals toward himself and toward one another within the human social process, and to bring that social process as a whole into his individual experience merely in these terms: he must also, in the same way that he takes the attitudes of other individuals toward himself and toward one another, take their attitudes toward the various phases or aspects of the common social activity . . . in which, as members of an organized society or social group, they are engaged. . . . This . . . is . . . the essential basis and prerequisite of the fullest development of the individual's self: only . . . [thus] does he develop a complete self or possess the sort of complete self he has developed (*MSS*, p. 154).

Imagination and the stage of play

Of course Mead argues that it is the vocal gesture which elicits responses shared with others and so allows the taking of the others' roles, the role-taking which constitutes play and which is organized and generalized in games. But we have rejected that argument, so it becomes important to see that his talk of the role-taking of play is easily assimilated by an account of the self which places imagination at the core of reflexivity. Children playing at being something other than they are – playing at being cowboys, playing at being sailors, playing bears – are engaged in conduct which would ordinarily be described as imaginative.

To extract the implications of this description we might recall, without, however, endorsing all the details of, Ryle's association of imagining and pretending. That association is in some quarters notorious, as Ryle is thought to have attempted a behaviouristic analysis of imagining, in terms of 'pretending', and that analysis is thought to be patently inadequate. But in *The Concept of Mind* Ryle makes no such attempt. He does try to draw parallels between pretending and imaging (visualizing a mountain or 'hearing' a tune in one's head, e.g.), claiming that each is a way of utilizing knowledge, that both might be grouped with a set of 'mock-actions [which] presuppose ingenuous actions, in the sense that performing the former involves, in a special sense, the thought of the latter.'[5] And, in arguing against the idea of a 'special Faculty of Imagination' and the idea that there is 'one nuclear operation in which imagination proper consists',[6] Ryle cites examples of pretending and notes that some of them could be indifferently described as 'fancying' or 'imagining'. He alludes to, in particular, some forms of children's play.

The self as an object of imagination

A child playing a cowboy surely is pretending to be a cowboy. He throws a rope around the garden stake, pretending to be lassoing a calf; he asks for some 'grub' at lunchtime and talks of his morning's adventures on the 'range'; he rides that backyard range on a broom he pretends is a horse, or he hops along, without even a broom, on a 'pretend horse' which, he might tell you, is a palomino. He is certainly employing imagination, and we might say that he is, insofar as he is able, playing the role of a cowboy. This seems uncontroversial.

Indeed, I risk spoiling the obviousness and ease of these claims by dwelling on them; but, if some tie is demanded between this case and topics previously broached, I can note that the child sees his cotton jumprope as a leather lasso, that he treats the garden stake as a calf to be branded, that he visualizes a prize palomino. And, if there is any resistance to taking these and other exercises of imagination through which the child pretends to be a cowboy to embody playing the role of a cowboy, it is likely to be felt by those who assume that to play the role of a cowboy one must really do what a cowboy does – one must ride a real horse and rope real calves. Connected with this assumption is the idea that – as this is what a man who works as a cowboy does – he, too, at work, fills the role of a cowboy. But if we insist that a real cowboy plays the role of a cowboy, we seem entranced by a thoroughly theatrical conception of human lives. And, besides, even one who would want to defend such a conception would have to grant that the examples Mead gives of role-playing, role-taking, are just those of children's play. So, fixing our focus on Mead's description of the first stage of self-development and on the task of showing how the description might accommodate an emphasis on imagination, we seem to face no obstacles.

We must not, however, overlook a warning entered by Mead: not yet living in a cultural atmosphere in which talk of the roles of everyday life, of roles in the lives of all men, women, and children, is common, perhaps too common (and being himself partly responsible for putting such talk in the air), Mead does characterize play as a 'process of taking the role of the other', but he says: 'the latter phrase is a little unfortunate because it suggests an actor's attitude which is actually more sophisticated than that which is involved. . . . To this degree it does not correctly describe that which I have in mind' (*MSS*, p. 161).

Now I have described this role-taking of play in terms of pretending and imagining, and Ryle wants to associate pretending and imagining precisely because he thinks they are, in some way, 'sophisticated':

> Pretending to growl like a bear, or lie still like a corpse, is a sophisticated performance, where the bear's growling and the corpse's immobility are naive.[7]
>
> Picturing [imagining] Helvellyn . . . stands in the same relation to seeing Helvellyn as sophisticated performances stand to those more naive performances, whose mention is obliquely contained in the description of the higher order performances.[8]

If Ryle's claim is not dismissed, must we assume that pretending and imagining, as 'sophisticated' acts, cannot, then, constitute the role-taking Mead is trying to describe? It might be thought that the sophistication Ryle is finding in these acts is not Mead's concern, so that the connotations Mead wants expunged from his notion of role-taking – the suggestions of the actor – could be plucked out and an idea still explainable in terms of pretending and imagining would remain. Ryle's ascriptions of sophistication and naivety are, after all, almost metaphorical; he is not here contrasting the stage actor and the child but trying to express his sense of a difference of 'logical type or category'. But Ryle and Mead are not simply talking past one another. And the intersection of their discussions is marked by a problem about self-consciousness.

Ryle thinks 'we use words like "play" and "pretend" for deliberate, concerted and rehearsed performances',[9] and deliberation, rehearsal, and the organization of a 'concerted' performance seem precisely the features Mead denies of the child's role-taking. Mead describes the infant and the very young child as slipping into and falling out of these roles, not 'utilising knowledge' to construct a fair representation of an other, not even spontaneously imitating the other, but simply exhibiting responses characteristic of the other because the other's attitude is also in the child, 'ready for expression' (*MSS*, p. 364). It is the stage actor who would give a deliberate, a concerted, a rehearsed performance, and this is just the sort of sophisticated action Mead does not have in mind.

But perhaps Ryle is wrong in his understanding of how we use the word 'pretend'. J. L. Austin says that in pretending 'there is

The self as an object of imagination

for preference an element of the extempore, and in the situation that prompts it an element of emergency. . . . True, there are "elaborate" pretences: but if there is too much of this, with making-up and dressing-up like an actor rather than a mimic or discuse, we begin to prefer to speak of, say, impersonation or imposture or disguise.'[10] Deliberation might indeed be necessary in order to produce a successful disguise, an impersonation or an imposture; and if 'we prefer to say that Col. Barker posed for twenty years as a man rather than that she pretended for twenty years',[11] we know this pose required concerted actions; and we do not think that children playing or pretending to be bears rehearse their performances.

But if Austin's remarks unsettle Ryle's, we find G. E. M. Anscombe rounding on Austin's emphasis on the pretending which is done through 'current personal performance' and which is basically impromptu. She points out that '[o]ne can pretend to be angry in a letter; . . . pretend through one's emissaries to come to an understanding with a foreign power.'[12] These pretenses certainly require some deliberation. These particular pretenses will be more successful as they are less impromptu, as they more completely control or suppress all elements of the extempore. And if these pretenses demand rather complicated controls, all pretending seems to require some self-conscious control. Anscombe says: '"Pretending" is an intention-dependent concept; one cannot pretend inadvertently.'[13]

This last claim would not be disputed by Austin or Ryle. But if some common ground is thus staked out, the boundary is clear and the distance is finally measured between Mead's position and the view that the child's role-taking involves pretending. Mead sees the responses which constitute the role the child plays as inadvertently aroused. He maintains that the child does not knowingly enact the part of the other: he or she just happens to stimulate himself or herself to the responses which are, or might be, called out in another. If this is how a child plays, plays at being another, then that play cannot be understood in terms of pretending. But is this sort of play really so unsophisticated? Doesn't the child in some sense set out to be a cowboy, or the teacher, or a bear? Doesn't the child intentionally play these roles; doesn't the child pretend?

Mead would have to grant this; but if it is insisted that the 'play'

The self as an object of imagination

which denotes his first stage of self-development must be understood as something like a technical term, so that we must, if we are to pursue his thought, follow him in excising the intention-dependency of playing at being another, we would encounter a serious difficulty. If the child is described as drifting into and out of the role of the other, neither trying to play it nor knowingly taking it, then there seems no reason to proclaim any progress toward individualization, toward delineation of a self. If the child is merely venting responses which are his own, 'ready for expression', and isn't producing them with some advertence to the fact that these responses are particularly characteristic of some other individual or type, then the child has not become an other for himself. The conceptual reward for taking the role of the other is supposed to be self-objectification: the other is for one an object, so if one plays the role of the other, one can be an object to oneself. But if the other is not for one an object, if the other is not antecedently distinguished from one's own subjectivity, then one does not achieve self-objectification in duplicating the other's response.

The idea now prevails that the infant or the very young child does not, in fact, distinguish himself from others or even from the external world. It is a tenet which is fundamental to J. M. Baldwin's theories of child psychology; it is a supposition elaborated by Freud (cf., e.g., 'Negation', *Standard Ed.*, 19, and 'Formulations on the Two Principles of Mental Functioning', *Standard Ed.*, 12); and Jean Piaget says, 'Every observer has noted that the younger the child, the less sense he has of his own ego. From the intellectual point of view, he does not distinguish between external and internal, subjective and objective.'[14] And of course, Mead, too, claims that the self is not there at birth, and basic to his developmental account is one variant of the idea that the human being does not initially distinguish himself from others but must come to do so.

The problem with an understanding of 'play' which denies its intentionality is not, then, that it is inconsistent with Mead's general approach. The problem is that this understanding leads us no closer to an account of the self or its development. It is not just that play, so construed, would not explain the generation of the self, that it would not itself constitute a mode of transformation equal to Mead's methodological aspirations, a mode which would

The self as an object of imagination

work the development of the self from biological or physiological material alone.[15] The problem is, rather, that this construal of 'play' seems descriptively unsatisfactory; if it is a technical construction, it is misshapen, awry. It would make no sense to lean on it, on this sort of 'play', as the first way station along the path of self-development, for it neither involves, nor requires, nor prompts any delineation of a self.

Knowingly enacting the role of another does, however, demand such delineation of a self. There must certainly be some sense of the difference between oneself and the other if one is to pretend to be that other. Some playing of a non-human role provides a clear illustration: the child playing bears, pretending to be a bear, knows he or she is not a bear. That is just why pretense and imagination are necessary. If the child simply had growling among his usual repertoire of reactions, if growling were just among the responses 'ready for expression'; if he were as likely as not to drop to the floor and pad about on all fours; then this growling, padding behavior would not be thought – by him or anyone else – to constitute a specific role-play. But the (normal) child who growls and pads and swipes with a hand held stiff from the shoulder, the child pretending to be a bear, does not normally exhibit this behavior, and that is just why it is appropriate to this pretending play, why the child has, so to speak, chosen it.

We have, then, a concept of play which involves, as Mead's concept does not, some contrast between self and other. And this must be Mead's fundamental desideratum, or he would not want to, would not be able to, designate play an achievement in taking the role of the other; it would not *be* what he says it is, a 'form of being another to one's self'. We can note, too, that this sort of play advances the apposition of self and other, and thus clarifies the differences between them, as some elements of the child's role-play are judged more effective than others. In pretending the child can be discovering which bits of behavior are most appropriate to the other and which are most characteristic of himself, for he must evidence or emphasize the former and suppress or disguise the latter. A more coherent sense of both himself and the other is thus obtained. Hence, as engaging in this sort of play does further demarcation of the self, it is reasonably cited in an explanation of the development of the self.

Pointing to this play is not, however, ultimately explicative of self-awareness. What I have insisted, after all, is that this play depends on there being some self-awareness, some knowledge of the distinction between self and other which is to be tried in playing the other's role. Accordingly, play cannot be certified as the source of self-awareness.

The necessity of that self-awareness notwithstanding, there is some overstatement in the claim that the child knowingly enacts the role of the other and some exaggeration in the idea that if the child does not know he or she is pretending, then he or she cannot be playing, playing at being another. The child can have lapses. Ryle speaks of 'the child playing bears, who knows, while in the well-lit drawing room, that he is only playing an amusing game, but feels faint anxieties when out on the solitary landing, and cannot be persuaded of his safety when in the darkness of a passage.'[16]

When the child suffers this increasing credulity we say his imagination has got the better of him. In this sort of case the child might have supported his role-playing with visions of shadowy dens and thoughts of gnashing teeth and the conflicts with other wild creatures; and now, dropping his own pretense of being a bear, he cannot dismiss those figments, though he is again fully inhabiting his human vulnerability. In other cases the sense of pretense can be lost as the child is caught up and remains in the role he or she is playing. And here, too, the transition might be described as a shift from his merely pretending to be, for example, a cowboy, to imagining that he is a cowboy. He abandons himself to the role and makes more or less full imaginative identification with the other, the other whose role he is taking.

These are moments of imaginative absorption, and it might be thought that, far from helping to build a coherent self, they imply some loss of self. Nonetheless, given their bracketing, their occurrence within the situation of play, these moments may support a deepening of the distinction between self and other. Within a context where, as I have argued, a contrast between the self and the other is presupposed, imaginative identification, which overcomes this contrast, can, in so doing, produce its significance. The child may feel at once both how much the same and how different it would be to be the other. (Or, to be the other as the child conceives him or her: it is not assumed that the child's conception of the other is the, or even a, true one.)

The self as an object of imagination

We have seen, then, that playing at being an other is an activity in which there can be imaginative identification with the other as well as the exercise of imagination in the furtherance of pretending; and we have seen that this play is understandably invoked in an account of the nature and the development of the self. Play of this sort actually is part of childhood and actually can contribute to the child's growth in self-awareness; and, moreover, this play can be seen to represent the process constitutive of the basic structure of the self – it is a form of being another to one's self. Must one go beyond this, however, to the stage Mead finds represented in games, if one is 'to develop a self in the fullest sense'?

Imagination and the stage of games: unification

This is, of course, Mead's contention: 'The game is an illustration of the situation out of which an organized personality arises' (*MSS*, p. 159). I will be less concerned with the illustrative adequacy of the game than with the personal organization and unity Mead wants to depict. This re-examination of Mead's remarks on play and game was prompted by the observation that a unified, a whole or complete self does not seem the object of the imaginative act of reflection. We need to ascertain the gravity of this fact. Does imagination fail to carry us to full self-possession, or is Mead misrepresenting our desired destination?

Mead says:

> The fundamental difference between [play and the game]* is that in the latter the child must have the attitude of all the others involved in that game. The attitudes of the other players which the participant assumes organize into a sort of unit, and it is that organization which controls the response of the individual (*MSS*, p. 151). *(The text, in an obvious misprint, reverses 'play and game'.)

That unit is the 'generalized other', and we can study its import for Mead not only by examining the details of the particular functions he assigns it, but also by pondering a more general question: Why must any organizing principle exist? Why is not the individual who can take the attitudes of various other individuals toward his or her words and deeds adequately self-reflective?

The self as an object of imagination
Imagination and the stage of games: autonomy

If we recall that self-reflection is enlisted in the service of self-control, we can see some motivation for a commitment to the idea of a generalized other. If one's behavior is always constrained by, and only by, the particular others with whom one is in contact, one might be thought to have no character of one's own. Full personal development and autonomy seem to require either transcendence or full and more or less permanent incorporation of the strictures imposed upon one by particular others. A man or woman whose attitudes shift to align with the attitudes of those who happen to be around him or her, whose personality changes radically to suit the views and expectations of other individuals, seems either not true to his or her own self, or devoid of a self with which to keep faith.

If there is, then, some reason to think that full self-development requires the establishment of a perspective, a point of reflection, which is not identical with, or as variable as, the viewpoints of particular other persons; there is, still, on the other hand, the fact that accommodation to others will be a part of the life of any well-adjusted human being. We might think that a sense of social propriety – an understanding, and a behaviorial conformity to the understanding, that the appropriateness of most statements and deeds varies with the time, the place, and the company – is one of the signal features of a more mature personality. William James is among those who endorse the idea that each person might develop a variety of 'social selves' ('Properly speaking, *a man has as many social selves as there are individuals who recognize him and carry an image of him in their mind*'), and he embraces the divisions in behavior which this conception of a set of selves implies:

> We do not show ourselves to our children as to our club-companions, to our customers as to the laborers we employ, to our masters and employers as to our intimate friends. From this there results what practically is a division of the man into several selves; and this may be a discordant splitting, as where one is afraid to let one set of his acquaintances know him as he is elsewhere; or it may be a perfectly harmonious division of labor, as where one tender to his children is stern to the soldiers or prisoners under his command.[17]

The self as an object of imagination

This conviction – that each of us is comprised of a variety of selves – is shared by many. Marcel Proust recites this same judgment, and it is evident that his agreement with James would extend to a confirmation of the root of our personal multiplicity: '. . . even in the most insignificant details of our daily life, none of us can be said to constitute a material whole, which is identical for everyone, and need only be turned up like a page in an account-book or the record of a will; our social personality is created by the thoughts of others.'[18]

But if James is content with the idea of a set of selves, if he is not concerned with unification of the self but only with the discord or the harmony of these practical divisions, Proust sometimes expresses chagrin at the disparate productions molded by social intercourse. He deplores 'the lie which seeks to make us believe that we are not irremediably alone, and which, when we talk to another person, prevents us from admitting that it is no longer we who speak, that we are fashioning ourselves in the likeness of strangers and not of our own ego . . .'.[19] Proust is concerned about the loss of authenticity in social interchange; he clearly believes there is an original self quite distinct from and easily neglected for the social selves given in and then embodying the attitudes and perspectives of others. Although this belief is far from consonant with Mead's theory of the self, Mead, too, is concerned that we not go on, past early childhood, in every conversation 'fashioning ourselves in the likeness of strangers'. We must at some point stand fast and exhibit our own character, each his or her own. We must cease to depend for our sense of self on the particular viewpoints of particular others and cease to play roles which suit these particular others. Mead seems to suggest that we can achieve this – we can cease to present ourselves as copies, finally *become* originals – only through the construction of the generalized other.

Mead says games are marked by 'regulated procedure' and 'rules' (*SW*, p. 285); he associates these regulations and rules which control the actions of the child in the game with the principles which guide the conduct of the fully self-conscious human being. The responses which are organized into the generalized other

> are abstract attitudes, but they constitute just what we term a

man's character. They give him what we term his principles. . . . He is putting himself in the place of the generalized other, which represents the organized responses of all members of the group. It is that which guides conduct controlled by principles, and a person who has such an organized group of responses is a man whom [*sic*] we say has character, in the moral sense (*MSS*, p. 163).

The adult who can take the attitude of the generalized other need not rely on any particular other to superintend his behavior; he is finally capable of determining and evaluating his own actions without reference to the particular views of any specific individual. The self, in thus being cut free from its dependence on a variety of particular others, is bound up into unity by these controlling abstract principles, and it becomes a coherent, autonomous whole.

It seems, then, that Mead insists on the unification of the self because he regards unification as concurrent, coadunate, with progression beyond particular dependencies and toward a condition of individual autonomy. But is autonomy achieved with the construction of the generalized other? It might be that one thus escapes the tyranny of particular others only to live under the more imposing rule of a more powerful and yet less congenial despot. Do we think self-rule consists of the incorporation of the general rules of the community at large? An individual who comes to be the incarnation of all the common attitudes might well be thought to have abdicated individual integrity. Mead identifies the mature man's principles as 'the acknowledged attitudes of all members of the community toward what are the values of that community' (*MSS*, p. 162). But a man or woman controlled by principles of this sort seems less than autonomous and more like an automaton. Giving up self-definition against the ragged variety of particular others, this man possesses a smooth, coherent self with a permanent structure, a structure built of 'attitudes . . . common to the group' (*MSS*, p. 162). But such an individual would surely strike us as excessively conventional. And if someone who measures his or her behavior by calibrations based on the views of particular others might be thought personally insecure; still, one might choose a circle of relevant others just because their attitudes impress one as worthy. One might heed these particular others just because, and only insofar as, their attitudes are

The self as an object of imagination

consonant with and reinforce one's deepest aspirations. Is the sway of a less fully individualized society to be preferred?

If Mead's theory seems to favor the production of a wholly conventional individual, we must note that Mead himself does not care to leave this social being devoid of an element of uniqueness or a capacity for nonconformist response. He says that 'we are not only what is common to all' (*MSS*, p. 163), and he introduces his distinction between the 'I' and the 'me' to accommodate spontaneity, novelty, and individual freedom. We must, then, examine that distinction, but before proceeding to that examination, let us pause to consider the spirit of his stipulation that the mature self be organized by a structure abstracted from the group.

FREEDOM AND SOCIAL CONTROL

In a paper entitled 'The Genesis of the Self and Social Control', published in the *International Journal of Ethics* of 1924–5, Mead presents a discussion of social control remarkable for its hygienic tone. Social control is dispassionately defined as 'bringing the act of the individual into relation with [the] social object [– i.e., the object of a social act]' (*SW*, p. 289), and it is said to depend 'upon the degree to which the individuals in society are able to assume the attitudes of the others who are involved with them in their common endeavor' (*SW*, p. 291). Mead is sanguine about increased social control and cautiously optimistic in his prognosis for its future, because it is for him just the way we 'bring people together' (*SW*, p. 292).

If it seems not to occur to Mead that people might not always care to be brought together with – into line with the attitudes of – all their fellows or that not all endeavors – common though they could be made to be – *ought* to be pursued, it is not because he values social order and efficiency to the exclusion of all else. Rather, he seems to believe in a sort of natural harmony between the inherent capacities, the intrinsic temper, of man and the society most fully controlled (that is, cooperative). It is not merely that man feels alienated only when social control begins to break down. Mead seems further to suppose that social control cannot be sustained unless the organization of society really is in tune with the humanity of its human members. He suggests that 'modern life', and the complexity of the interconnections through which one lives in the twentieth century, are explicable only on that supposition: though the construction of the generalized other allows us to abstract the uniformities in the diverse responses of 'numberless others', still,

> the number of different responses that enter into our social conduct seems to defy any capacity of any individual to assume the roles which would be essential to define our social objects. And yet, though modern life has become indefinitely more complex than it was in earlier periods of human history, it is far easier for the modern man than for his predecessor to put himself in the place of those who share with him the functions of government, or join with him in determining prices. It is not the number of participants, or even the number of different functions, that is of primary importance. The important question is whether these various forms of activities belong so naturally to the member of a human society that, in taking the role of another, his activities are found to belong to one's own nature (*SW*, p. 291).

If the quasi-empirical claims about the social ease and the shared participations of 'the modern man' strike us as a bit quaint, perhaps even, ironically, socially isolated or naive, nonetheless we cannot, I think, accuse Mead of a fundamental insensitivity to the issue of conflict between the individual and society. Although he presents the individual as formed by the community, he views society as the organic outgrowth of human possibilities. He seems to suggest that a well-functioning society cannot fail to be human, that the social structure will not be accepted by, will not work to shape the selves of, the community unless it does reinforce each individual's personal authenticity. And he is confident that when a conflict between an individual and a basically sound community does occur, the mechanism of its resolution is structurally equivalent to the mechanism of ordinary interactions.

> The only way we can react against the disapproval of the entire community is by setting up a higher sort of community. . . . A person . . . may stand out by himself . . . against [his community]. But to do that he has to speak with the voice of reason to himself. He has to comprehend the voices of the past

The self as an object of imagination

and of the future [– a larger community]. That is the only way . . . the self can get a voice which is more than the voice of the [particular] community (*MSS*, p. 168).

But in fact Mead's theory reserves for each person another voice which is more, or other, than the voice of the community.

THE 'I' AND THE 'ME' AND NOVELTY

Along with and responding to the social 'me', that organized set of the attitudes of the community, there is an 'I', an element of spontaneity and personal novelty.

> Together they constitute a personality as it appears in social experience. The self is essentially a social process going on with these two distinguishable phases. If it did not have these two phases there could not be conscious responsibility, and there would be nothing novel in experience (*MSS*, p. 178).

The 'I' is subjectivity; it is never an object in experience, except as 'a historical figure' (*MSS*, p. 174): The distinct phases of 'I' and 'me' are available as objects in memory, but, then, the 'I' of the past is given as a 'me', a 'me' which has superseded or been added to the 'me' which was its contemporaneous counterpart.[20] As an 'I', however, this element of the self is a principle of uncertainty. Mead stresses the impossibility of predicting its actions; he says that the individual himself never knows quite what he himself will do:

> . . . how we will act never gets into experience until after the action takes place (*MSS*, p. 177).
> If he says he knows what he is going to do, even there he may be mistaken. He starts out to do something and something happens to interfere. The resulting action is always a little different from anything which he could anticipate (*MSS*, p. 177).

But if this is the novelty associated with the 'I', the 'I' seems unlikely to provide a 'sense of freedom, of initiative' (*MSS*, p. 177). Mead describes the actions and reactions of the 'I' as unpredictable and virtually irrepressible, and he supports this description with an understanding of overt human action as always somehow haphazard, always somewhat surprising even to the actor. The spontaneity of the 'I' seems too completely uncontrolled. Mead's theory saves the individual from stifling conventionality only by allowing him or her the not fully satisfying indulgence of random acts.

Now the account of the self centered on imagination was never suspected of leading inexorably to the construction of individuals definable as abstractions from the attitudes common to all. It has thus no comparable pressing need for the distinction between the 'I' and the 'me' as a rescue device and, so, need not face the task of making the distinction more suitable for the salvage operation.[21]

We should note in passing, however, that insofar as there are phases in the structure of the self described by this account, too, they do not sort into the energetic but empty subjectivity and the inert if expanding objectivity of Mead's 'I' and 'me'. The object of the imaginative act can be itself a spur to action. The ways in which one sees oneself are pervaded by motivating affect. The effects of such affect will of course vary – from one kind of imaginative apprehension to another, from person to person, from one moment to the next. (If I today see myself as dull, I may shrink from certain company and conversations, afraid my dullness will be found out and despised. If tomorrow I see myself as dull, I may decide to seek taxing social engagements, determined to hone my personality through extraordinary efforts. If you today see yourself as sharp-tongued, you may shrink from certain company and conversations, afraid that your sharpness will be found out and despised . . . This variability is not, however, utterly haphazard, and within a given individual and for particular classes of reflective judgments, there may well be discernible patterns of objective responsibility: A great range and variety of conduct may yet be comprehensible as the repercussive activity of the object grasped by imaginative self-reflection.

We can find, then, in contrast with Mead's unpredictable 'I', a source of action which, if not operating by simple, obvious, or predetermined mechanisms, is, nonetheless, moving the individual along courses which we know to be common, which we take to be intelligible, methodical, organized. We can see in the phases of the self of imagination both more activity and, curiously, more stability.

Mead introduces the 'I' as, in part, the agent of personal novelty and caprice. It is thus also worth noting, again in passing, that imagination might most naturally be identified as the expedient which can take us beyond conventions or out of the social roles we happen to inhabit. It seems the instrument which can implement a coherent yet creative transport. To make plain the credibility of this claim or, rather, to elaborate this remark into a description full enough to warrant credence, we must attend to the circumstances which provoke the imaginative apprehension of the self as well as to problems about the notion of creativity. Such an elaboration must be postponed, however, as there is one last aspect of Mead's characterization of the 'I' which must be noted and then linked to the larger discussion of the unity of the self.

THE 'I' AND HABITS

Mead also identifies the 'I' with 'the biologic individual' (*MSS*, pp. 370–3), the creature of flesh, blood, bones and organs, the seat of impulses, the source of reactions and responses. That identification would seem to set some bounds on the randomness of the 'I'. Biology is in fact too easily understood teleologically, and if the 'I' is the biological organism it can readily, if with some dangers of distortion, be seen as orderly and not without its own purposes. Among the uniformities which could be mentioned even without any glossing of, or glossing over, contemporary scientific theory are those called 'habits'. A human being's habits are, of course, socially shaped; some are the result of pointed social training. They are, nonetheless, molded on or into a biological organism with a limited, if great and indefinite and not wholly determined, plasticity. Mead himself does find an occasion to describe the biologic individual in terms of 'habits of response' and to imply that self-development involves the reorganization of, or the construction of new, habits of response (*MSS*, p. 371).

Now, if the biologic individual can be understood as a set of habits, and if the biologic individual is identical with the 'I', and the 'I' is identified as an element of the self, then the self should be understood as at least partially constituted by a set of habits. But Mead frequently tries to distinguish the self from habits. He says that 'our habitual actions [do not involve a self, but] . . . experience . . . [which does not take] place in relationship to the

The self as an object of imagination

self' (*MSS*, p. 135). The self is 'distinct from a group of habits. . . . [Most of] the sets of habits which we have . . . mean nothing to us . . .' (*MSS*, p. 163).

Mead's desire to detach habits from the self he wants to describe is puzzling. Others often think they come to know us as they become acquainted with out habits; and if asked to characterize us, to describe not just the statistics of physical appearance or our place in the social and economic world, but us – our very selves – they would surely draw on a knowledge of our habits of action and expression. Indeed, a portrayal which was not only based on this knowledge of habits, but was rendered strictly in terms of this material could be both extremely full and finely shaded. A rich description would report subtle details of characteristic behavior or would disclose large patterns of life – habitual tempers or tendencies. The direction and the accuracy of such a portrayal would seem to depend only on the intimacy of acquaintance and the perspicacity of the portraitist. A keen and close companion could certainly offer an illuminating representation, drawing only on the idea of, simply delineating, one's habits.

But on what is this companion shedding light? Features distinct from and not involving the self? This would seem to be Mead's opinion, and this seems quite implausible. And the claim that the companion's description cannot be touching the self because it is a tracing of mere outer appearances – features necessarily external to the self – this claim is decidedly forbidden to Mead. Central to his thought, after all, is the contention that the self is a social object. That its existence as a social object is tied to a kind of public accessibility can be made plain if we explore one last region of his belief in the generalized other.

I want to do that now, to propose and then examine one more motivation to accept the idea of the generalized other and the unity of self it is supposed to guarantee. This new understanding of Mead's desiderata can then be related to, can emphasize the peculiarity of, Mead's severance of habits from the self. A path will then be cleared for a discussion of the place of habit in an explanation of the self centered on imagination.

THE GENERALIZED OTHER AND THE SCIENTIFIC PERSPECTIVE

We have considered one possible motivation for the view that maturation, complete self-development, requires the construction of a generalized other, and that motivation was uncompelling. Although the whimsical adoption of roles may be connected with immaturity, and a shifting dependence on the particular attitudes of particular others may indicate an insecure sense of self or inadequate self-possession, defining oneself against or in terms of the generalized other is not the most attractive remedy for these deficiencies. There may be a gain in consistency, but there seems no greater autonomy, no real gain in self-governance, when one adopts and lives by the attitudes common to all. We have seen that in Mead's theory maturity seems constrictively bound to conventionality.

Perhaps, however, the spirit of the conventions of the generalized other has been misread. It has appeared to be dully overbearing and oppressive to individuality, but perhaps its force is of a piece with the hardness of facts. And perhaps it can be liberating, just as truth is said to have the power to make us free. There is reason to believe that Mead would want to identify the viewpoint of the generalized other with the impersonal viewpoint of science and to argue, then, that only with, from, the viewpoint of the generalized other can one discover the truth of one's self.

The threads of Mead's thoughts on metaphysics and epistemology are spun from the same fiber as his thoughts on psychology and sociology, and they are all tightly woven into a continuous fabric: The generalized other is the organization of the attitudes of others, and it is built by abstracting what is common to all; its perspective, Mead says, is the one an individual must adopt if the individual is to develop a full, an integrated self. This unified self will emerge, will appear as the object of reflection, only when the point of view taken is that derived from the organization of what is common to all. Compare with this theory Mead's remark on scientific knowledge and its object: '. . . [A] selection of characters [features, properties] which are identical for all experience, or nearly so, and are identical for all individuals gives us the scientific object. They constitute an object of knowledge.'[22]

Charles W. Morris, the editor of *Mind, Self, and Society* and

The Philosophy of the Act, says that for Mead 'knowledge consists of the process of co-ordinating perspectives' (*PA*, p. xlix). But Mead is not entirely unambiguous on this topic. He does claim that sense perception involves the coordination of perspectives. Visual experience, for example, is organized into the perception of objects only as there is an identification of visual and contact dimensions in the 'field of congruence' marked by actual manipulation. He speaks of the baby 'mapping . . . his environment' (*PA*, p. 134), crawling about, his visual experience varying with time as he moves through space until eventually he reaches and handles an object. This coordination of perspectives is achieved as one phase of the experience of the act becomes dominant and controls the others. The controlling phase is always that of manipulation. The example of the penny which is seen to be round, though it is 'presented to the eye as an oval or a line', leads Mead to remark:

> The problem which is involved in this . . . perception is that it cannot be accounted for by a mere fusing of one content with another. One cannot fuse an oval with a circle. Nor is it a mere substitution in which the visual deliverance of one retina is substituted for that of [another.] . . . [Rather,] our percept of the penny is . . . in terms of the action under the conditions of most advantageous conduct. . . . We act toward it as round (*PA*, pp. 127–8).

Perception does, then, according to Mead, require the rankings, the adjustments, which might be called 'coordination'. But Mead denies that the percept is the object of knowledge. He wants to identify knowledge with the movement of – the solution of problems in – scientific research. (Cf. *PA*, pp. 89–95.) And when Mead describes the field in which the scientist works, he speaks less of the coordination than of the 'intersection' of perspectives. He suggests that the scientist's job is to encompass these intersecting perspectives: the wasp has one perspective, the fig tree another. But some events in the life-histories of the wasp and the tree can be seen from either perspective. Here the two perspectives intersect. The wasp gathers honey and the flowers of the fig tree are pollinated. Moments such as these 'constitute a sort of plane of events which is identical in the two perspectives. The events that precede and succeed the identical events in the two perspectives do not coincide. The succession in the fig tree is the fertilization of the flower, that in the wasp is the digestion of the honey' (*PA*, p. 184). There is continuation in two separate perspectives. But a human being can take a view which encompasses both perspectives, and the pomologist will do so.

This description of the perspective of the scientist has clear affinities with some of Mead's comments on the generalized other. The scientist abstracts from the life-histories of the insect and the plant and constructs a 'plane of events'. This is a unified dimension which exists for him or her only; it does not exist as a plane in the wasp's or the tree's perspective; it is wholly a product of the scientist's abstraction and synthesis. Similarly, the generalized other, abstracted from the intersection of the attitudes of particular others, constitutes a synthetic whole directed (as is its attitudinal nature) on a likewise synthetic whole, the object self. Just as one takes the view of the generalized other to gain a perspective in which the unified self appears, the scientist takes a perspective which unifies an object of knowledge:

> To the biologist there is a common environment of an anthill or of a beehive, which is rendered possible by the intricate social relationships of the ants and the bees. It is entirely improbable that this perspective exists in the perspectives of individual ants or bees . . . (*SW*, p. 312).

But neither does the perspective of the individual ant or bee exist in the perspective of the biologist. Mead says that the perspective of the scientist 'includes' (*PA*, p. 184) the perspectives of the ants and the bees, the wasp and the fig tree, but in fact it supplants them. They are not retained as parts of a whole. They do not go together to make up a larger perspective; they cannot, just as the circle and the oval of the penny cannot, be fused. The scientific point of view which Mead describes is not a point of view which comprises all others; rather, it is a point preferable to others, just as, for him, the perspective of the generalized other is to be preferred to particular perspectives on the self.

In a discussion of the ultimate perspective of the physical sciences, Mead makes a number of remarks on what he takes to be the advantage of the scientific viewpoint:

> The most that physical science seems to accomplish . . . is to free our perceptions and analyses of them from the

idiosyncrasies and perspectives of particular observers. It finds uniformities which hold for all observers and thinkers. It does not transcend the fundamental condition of contact observation itself (*PA*, p. 22).

The ultimate experience of contact is not subject to the divergencies of distance experience. It is that into which every perspective can be translated (*PA*, p. 281).

In the scientific account we attempt to approach a level of nature in which the organism and the object are at an instant, and are recognized in their reality, i.e., their contact character, and those other characters which they maintain unchanged in the manipulatory area. It is the area of congruence, of substitution and measurement (*PA*, p. 104).

We may leave aside the question of whether the physicist's account of reality is still grounded in what Mead calls 'the ultimate experience of contact'. We are interested in deciding whether the parallel within Mead's thought between the viewpoint of science and the viewpoint of the generalized other is worth preserving, whether, given this understanding of science, Mead has good reason to suppose that the attitude of the generalized other must be adopted if one is to ascertain the reality of the self. I think we can find good reason to abandon this parallel. The crucial obstacle is a difference in the natures of the objects surveyed from those two viewpoints, or a difference in our interests in their natures.

Mead says that in science 'we attempt to approach' an 'abstract' level of nature, 'the fiction of the world at an instant' (*PA*, p. 111). This abstraction is appropriate because we want to describe something like the *type* of an object: the history of a given atom is not a locus of interest; we do not seek to understand it – its individuality and uniqueness – for its own sake; this atom is understood as representative of, interchangeable with, its kind, even as the delineation of the kind is recognized as a scientific problem. To begin to solve this problem, according to Mead's theory of science, we must find a viewpoint with the proper focus, a focus at the intersection of all differing perspectives on the object so that uniformities, the object's typical features, are disclosed.

But if this is the viewpoint we want to take in science, because our interest is in the type of an object, this is surely not the

The self as an object of imagination

viewpoint appropriate to our interest in selves – unless, of course, we are attempting a science of the self. Scientific psychology aside, our everyday interest in the self is secured in an interest not in typical but in particular persons and their particular peculiarities. We surely do best, in contemplating the heart of another, to regard that other as a perfectly particular being and not as just a representative or interchangeable type. Now if this is how we should study another, should we do otherwise when we take ourselves as others, when we make our selves the objects of reflection?

This is not to say that we should not expect some unanimity in our views of ourselves and others; and such harmony might be wrought by our grasp on the real uniformities and the patterns in the lives of the objects of our observation. But there is a difference between looking at a pattern in the life of a particular human being and regarding the life of that human being as the instantiation of a particular pattern. The glance of the generalized other, if it is assimilated to the view Mead attributes to science, would find an individual only as a type. Unity of self would be procured, and social accessibility insured, for this viewpoint stands at the intersection of all particular viewpoints; but the cost would be too dear. And there is no need to pay it.

HABITS AND THE SELF

If Mead is concerned to mark, with one stroke, a factor involved in the development of the human being from infancy through childhood and a feature of persons which is in principle accessible to any well-placed observer, he would do well to reconsider his treatment of habit. In urging the necessity of the generalized other as a unifying principle and insisting on the developmental stages of play and game, Mead says that

> the situation of play where there is a simple succession of one role after another . . . is, of course, characteristic of the child's own personality. The child is one thing at one time and another at another, and what he is at one moment does not determine what he is at another. That is both the charm of childhood as well as its inadequacy. You cannot count on the child; you

The self as an object of imagination

cannot assume that all the things he does are going to determine what he will do at any moment. He is not organized into a whole. The child has no definite character, no definite personality (*MSS*, p. 159).

There is no need to assent to the last claim – that the child has no personality – and it is not clear that we can or want to find a mechanism which will 'determine' an adult's actions. But there is no doubt that the mutability which both delights and distresses Mead is often lost as the regularities of habits become firmly fixed. The fluidity of childhood may be frozen, then, not by the glance of the generalized other, but by the solidifying force of habit.

And, as I remarked earlier, it is also true that our habits are accessible to others, that others can and often do identify us in terms of these habits. Thus, some of the work of stabilizing, unifying and identifying for which Mead recruits the generalized other is taken in the stride of habit. But the puzzle remains: why, given the ease with which the notion of habit steps into the framework Mead sets out, why does Mead want to bar any connection between self and habits?

The answer is that there remains, for Mead, a problem about accessibility. He would not deny that others can discern our habits. The difficulty is rather with individual self-awareness. Though Mead makes few explicit statements on habit, he is evidently convinced of the basic soundness of some aspects of a pragmatic account of its features and functions. James says that 'habit diminishes the conscious attention with which our acts are performed.'[23] And he emphasizes the utility of this: it in fact enlarges our capacity for intelligent action; as our habitual actions proceed automatically, with less effort of choice and care required to sustain the sequence of performance, consciousness is freed to mediate the still unsettled and troublesome aspects of our environment. But if James points to the mechanism of habit as a stabilizing and potentially liberating structure in a creature capable of learning and of organizing its behavior, Mead must regard the lack of consciousness with which habitual actions can be performed as the deficiency which impedes the inclusion of habits in an entity whose defining trait is awareness of itself. The self is an object to itself, but our habits are not objects of our attention; hence they are not parts of our selves. This must be the thinking which underlies Mead's overstatement: 'We all of us have . . . certain groups of habits, such as the particular intonation which a person uses in his speech. This is a set of habits of vocal expression which one has but which one does not know about'; the conclusion: these habits 'mean nothing to us' (*MSS*, p. 163).

This claim is startling because, even if habits are understood to establish actions requiring diminished conscious attention, it does not follow that we do not know of the establishment of the habit. And Mead's usual pattern of theorizing would suggest that we should eventually become aware of our habits. For if we say that, as we do not know of our habits, they mean nothing to us, we can never deny that they can mean a great deal to those around us. Even the example Mead chooses – a habit of intonation in speech – an example presumably chosen because he takes the habit to be insignificant – is not without its effect on those around us and so on the course and nature of our social interchanges. To sketch the point crudely: people may avoid the whiner; disregard the sense of a soft, diffident speech; submit grudgingly to the growler. If we want to smooth our social relations and to be in control of and take responsibility for more of our actions and their effects, we must come to grasp our habits.

Mead should accept this – it is in keeping with the trend of his thinking on individual and societal development. But he is restricted by the confining boundaries of his own map of habits: he seems to draw his line of inclosure around just some absent-minded performances and some of the elements of which one is unaware in conscious or deliberate acts. He seems to ignore John Dewey's distinction between routine and intelligent habit, and Dewey's reminder that automatic techniques can be employed with conscious skill, that the mechanism of habit can be 'fused with thought and feeling'.[24] His neglect of Dewey on this topic is quite surprising, and not just because of the closeness of their professional lives. The real curiosity in this context is the virtual identity of their theories of reflection and deliberation, which they both describe as involving the reorganization of habit.[25] For if Mead can admit that the human being, from childhood on, can self-consciously arrest impulsive responses by shifting attention to, and analyzing, his or her own habitual reactions, then there is finally no reason for him to distinguish habits from the content of the self.

The self as an object of imagination

And if he can say that reflection on habit includes 'representation, . . . holding out the imagery of the results of various actions' (*MSS*, p. 368), can say that 'images . . . serve the function . . . in man's mind of reconstructing both objects and habits' (*MSS*, p. 373), then there is finally no reason for him to reject an account of the self centered on imagination. If imagination can be employed, then nothing prevents us from attending to our own habits, from seeing (hearing, etc.) ourselves acting in those habits.

Nothing prevents us, but, of course, nothing insures us. Whether or not we will notice our habits, which of them we will discover, is, in part, a function of our social context. Mead and Dewey suggest that the imaginative rehearsal of habitual actions can be occasioned by a conflict, disunity in the impulses aroused in a situation or a clash between an impulse and an environmental obstacle. Friction with companions could also spark the imagination. To return to a rough example already set: the winces and the escapes of others could lead one to reflect and to hear oneself as a whining complainer. But there need not be overt social conflict; there need only be some engagement with others. In fact, in some company, the absence of an open struggle could lead one to reflect and, for example, to see oneself as spineless, as an habitual coward.

IMAGINATION AND THE SOCIAL SELF

Facing these sorts of cases, we should be struck once again by the social dimension of imagination. The self may not be given in a response which is immediately shared by others – that was Mead's doctrine and we rejected it; but there must be a foundation of shared responses to support the vault of imagination. The whining complainer, for example, must share winces with the others. He need not, of course, now or ever react with a wince to his own tone. *Pace* Mead, we need not duplicate the behavior of others at the moment of sighting ourselves in reflection. But if the complainer shares the winces in another, a larger, context, then the wince on the face of the other can mean something to him now. And it might occasion an imaginative grasp of a feature of himself as the provocation.

The self as an object of imagination

Or it might not. Even resting on the shared foundation of our language and holding another's explicit comments on some bit of our behavior and his reactions to it – he tells us we have once again exhibited our annoying habit of complaining – we can fail to realize that bit of behavior in imagination. We might fail, or we might refuse, to grasp, to see, that behavior – or larger, more complex stretches of our lives – as this other tells us he did. The possibility of such failures and refusals does not, however, tell against the claim that the self is a social object. Such disaccord may instead mark the bounds, or influence the future, of our social community.

A sense of community is sometimes thought to depend on a kind of mutual knowledge. Ideal communities, utopias, are often small, in part so that one will know and be known by one's neighbors. Such personal knowledge sometimes seems a requirement for both harmonious social relations and the satisfaction of the individual. I want to explore an equation of the knowledge of persons and a sort of social harmony or concord. To begin to do this, and to begin to develop the import of this view of the self as a construct of imagination, I shall turn some attention toward the topics of self-knowledge, self-deception, and egocentricity.

The picture of the self which has been developed through the preceding discussion shows the skeleton of Mead's social self. It is essentially reflexive and, though the mechanism of reflection is not the vocal gesture but imagination, ties between this mechanism and the social process have been maintained. What has been discarded is the generalized other and, with it, the idea that the whole of the self must be caught in reflection. Unification of the self need not be an inevitable theoretical problem, if only we do not first think of the human body as a collection of parts; and if only we admit that we do not need a unitary object to produce a unified object, that a variety of forces can work toward a single shape; and if only we remember that habits integrate vast regions of our lives.

We need not, then, find a theoretical problem; but perhaps there is a moral problem. If the whole of the self is not an object of reflection, isn't self-deception encouraged? If we recognize no requirement for a full awareness of all elements of the self, don't we diminish our sense of human responsibility? We must consider the implications of this account of the self.

4
PROBLEMS OF THE SELF

SELF-DECEPTION

If what is begun as a simple description of the self sketches a pattern which suggests that the finished picture will portray the self of bad faith, a self marked by self-deception, then there might be two very different responses to the sketch. One would be to reject it, to dismiss it as a drawing which does not render the proper subject. The model, after all, should be the model self, and this is the authentic, the pure self. Everyone knows that particular selves may be found at various removes from the ideal, and we may be interested in depicting these lapses; but if we are to do this we must first possess a sense of the standard, the exemplary self.

That could be one reaction. Another, springing from an impression of the ubiquity of self-deception, would be to respect and accept the sketch as a piece of realism. If all individuals are self-deceived, then any picture of the self which does not reflect the inevitability of this condition has not been accurately traced. As the self is always in bad faith, a true paradigm will display this character.

While the representation of the self which has been taking shape throughout the preceding discussion does not incorporate bad faith as essential from the start, and it does not insist that bad faith will form the final mold, it does have contours likely to attract those inclined to grant the usualness of self-deception. However, it does not necessarily credit the correctness of their perception. Rather, the virtue of this account is that, without containing any presumption that most people *are* in a blameworthy state of bad faith, it can offer some support for, and explanation of, the surfacing of the sentiment *that* they are, for the *feeling* of omnipresent self-deception.

And this sentiment deserves some scrutiny. We need no reminder that the notion of self-deception is quite puzzling: the idea of lying to oneself, of being immediately both victim and perpetrator of a lie, of knowing a truth and yet hiding it from oneself is indeed an idea both superficially and deeply puzzling. And, were they not so common, the commonness of attributions of self-deception would perhaps seem puzzling too. Is it not curious that people are so comfortable with this paradox, that there is so little reluctance to employ a concept which seems so obviously incoherent?

Moreover, although it could certainly be claimed that this is exactly what we should expect, the ratio between, on the one hand, third- and second-person attributions and, on the other, first-person ascriptions can sometimes seem astonishing. Of course truly saying or thinking 'I am self-deceived (about X)' is impossible. But there is one's past to consider: and shouldn't one who finds bad faith in others expect to discover it with approximately equal frequency in his or her own history? And shouldn't one who thinks self-deception extremely prevalent naturally assume that he or she too is undoubtedly presently self-deceived, and shouldn't he or she then be left in wonder and anxiety? It is true that some people are very concerned with the self-deception in their own pasts. And it is true that some people are anxious and do wonder about their own present self-deceptions. And it is also true that some people can accept a general imputation of their own bad faith and still feel no confoundment, just as anyone might accept the idea that others do not always tell one the truth and yet not feel a constant urgency to hound out lies. But conceding all that, there is still an imbalance which can seem discomfiting, an imbalance which we might prefer to see stabilized in some explanation. If I revert to a topic of earlier discussion – Mead's remarks on the coordination of perspectives – my approach to these problems will not be direct, but neither will it be long or circuitous.

Earlier, against a claim by Charles Morris and in search of a parallel along whose lines I could motivate part of Mead's attachment to the concept of the generalized other, I drew attention to some of Mead's comments on science. The doctrines presented were that the scientific viewpoint is one which includes or encompasses a variety of perspectives and that the object of scientific knowledge is located at the intersection of all perspectives. Sometimes, however, Mead does suggest a somewhat different story of the progress of the scientific viewpoint. It does not move constantly 'outward' to take in an ever larger field of particular views, nor does it move steadily 'inward' to the point where all perspectives converge. It has no impetus of its own at all. It is, rather, propelled by the engine of the functioning community. The growth, the development, the very life of the community gives rise to particular problems. It is from the point of these problems – these specific and unpredictable problems – that the vector of the scientific perspective must spring. Objectivity is always provisional, and it always provides transport through or around a particular impasse encountered by the active community or by an individual member of the community.

An individual's perspective is not inherently subjective; it is only so labelled if it cannot be coherently organized with the working viewpoint of the community, if it exists in, and suggests no solution to or resolution of, conflict with that larger, antecedently operating perspective. Mead accepts as a 'natural fact' (cf. *PA*, p. 613) that 'a dominant common perspective . . . claims the individual', and he explains the vitality of this perspective in this way:

> [T]he passage of the landscape is in the perspective of the passenger as taking place in the common perspective of all the occupants of the train, of all who are in that consentient set, but the consentient set of those without the train triumphs over that of those within the train because it organizes more completely and successfully the processes which are constitutive of the selves involved in the whole act. The separate perspective of the man within the train, with its aspect of nature as a whole, hangs there as a defeated hypothesis, not in consciousness but in a nature which includes minds as essential parts. The distinction

between the defeated hypothesis and the successful hypothesis of the landscape at rest within which the train moves does not lie in the greater objectivity of the latter perspective, so far as immediate experience is concerned, but in the experimental results of acting upon the two. Both consentient sets are there in nature, but one set only can maintain itself in the conduct of the community (*PA*, p. 610).

This conception of the organization or coordination of perspectives may seem to suffer in Mead's illustration of it. What are the experimental results which would defeat the perspective of the passenger? It seems any datum could be located from either perspective, and that it could be taken from its place in one perspective to its place in the other by an orderly transformation; for, with the appropriate set of tools, the right equations, the viewpoint of the passenger and the viewpoint of one outside the train are reciprocally reconstructible. Nonetheless, it is true that the community maintains a perspective in which the train is moving. Is this just because there are more people outside the train than in? Mead says that when the common perspective is accepted it 'is not a case of the surrender to a vote of the majority, but the development of another self through . . . intercourse with others . . .' (*SW*, p. 316).

If we do not accept Mead's assertion that experimental results can always and definitively decide between these two perspectives, then Mead never seems to secure his contention that 'one [perspective or] set [of perspectives] only can maintain itself in the conduct of the community.' But we might grant that there would be unnecessary complications in the thoughts of an occasional passenger who would insist when in the train that the landscape moves and not the train and insist, when watching the train from a hotel window, that the train moves and not the land. Someone born and living a lifetime on a constantly moving train would, however, have no reason to doubt the fixity of his or her own position. It seems that it is only because passengers embark and disembark at depots, and mingle with those who – do in fact themselves – live on the land, that the land-based perspective 'maintains itself in the conduct of the community'. And Mead is right: this perspective does not prevail through majority rule; the train passenger does not find himself outvoted at the station. But the community lives on stable ground.

The problem with the idiosyncratic view is not that it is idiosyncratic; it might see past a problem which has confronted the community; it might, after all, be a revelation. But if this is the claim of a particular perspective, that a veil has been drawn back, interest can be maintained only if something really is disclosed, only if a discovery actually is exhibited. And *that* people *will* want, will come, to see. This is the pragmatic moral of Mead's story. The individual perspective is rejected, becomes a defeated hypothesis, only if it does not work. If it can be fitted into an already functional perspective (or set of perspectives), or if it is in itself so useful that it can rival the practical successes of that other perspective (or set), then it will be preserved 'in the conduct of the community'.

I shall not try to decide whether or not there is here the germ of a sustainable theory of knowledge, whether or not there is here the adumbration of a reasonable general account of objectivity. I want only to draw some strands of this thought back to the problem of self-deception. The cable I want to construct would connect attributions of self-deception with breakdowns or difficulties in the organization of perspectives; I want to suggest that ascriptions of self-deception mark evident tensions between, typically, an individual's and the community's perspectives.

The self-reflective act of imagination was said to involve an attempt at something like the perception of another. There is no real distance between that idea of reflection and the idea of the achievement of a perspective. One sees oneself as (X) from a particular point of view. A particular interpretation proceeds from and so discloses a particular perspective.

We have also noted that the imaginative apprehension of the self need not be considered exhaustive: in these moments of reflection one may grasp the self as a whole without grasping the whole of the self. That fact might be thought to underlie the possibility of self-deception. If one can see oneself as x, and as y, and as z, and as x', and so on, and one need never work these interpretations into a unified whole, then one always has the option of neglecting or avoiding some interpretations. The whole self might be thought of as a mosaic, the particular interpretations as the bits of inlay: imaginative reflection produces a variety of distinct objects. But when these discrete objects are laid next to one another, relationships are established and the whole combination presents a picture which is not there in the mere aggregation, or piling together, of the parts. If half the pieces are missing, however, or if the given pieces are improperly arranged, no picture or a picture quite different from a true portrayal will emerge. If, then, an individual never takes all the appropriate perspectives on himself, he will never see his true self; an incomplete, a bad, perhaps a deceptive sense of his self, his behavior and his engagements with others and the world, will obtain.

There is undoubtedly a problem which can be highlighted with this illustration, but it is not clearly the problem, or the paradigm problem, of self-deception. What is not illuminated is the element of willfulness. We take a self-deceiver's ignorance to be intentional. He seems not simply missing some of the pieces required to present a true picture; he seems to be suppressing or hiding them.

Accounts of self-deception rendered in terms of belief often fail at just this point and in an analogous way. If the self-deceiver is described as one who holds inconsistent or incompatible beliefs, the special puzzle of self-deception is lost; or, rather, self-deception is not captured in the description, as its puzzle has not been found: Who but a Descartes would think possible the task of sorting out all of his or her beliefs? We unabashedly admit that we do not know the whole range and all the implications of our beliefs; and we are not all of us good enough logicians to be sure that we would recognize inconsistencies among the beliefs of which we are aware.

For a similar reason self-deception is not distinguished as the cement in a faulty structure of beliefs and evidence. Holding onto a belief in the face of good evidence against it, or refusing to accept a proposition despite good evidence for it, is common enough if only for the reason that evidence is often difficult both to discern and to judge. We must not forget the variety and the dimensions of human incapacities and failures. Even in cases where an individual is not baffled by, or ignorant of, what counts as evidence for a belief but nonetheless does not bring his or her beliefs into line with this evidence – say he or she sees the evidence against p and sees that it is good evidence, and yet still believes p – or in cases where the contradictory nature of two beliefs is made plain to an individual, but nonetheless the individual refuses to relinquish either belief; we do not always describe these aberrations as self-deceptive. People may be incoherent in divers ways.

The locus of the incoherency of self-deception is not, I think, wholly within the individual. We should look instead at points of conflict between an individual's perspective, an individual's interpretation of himself or herself, and the community's perspective, the community's view of that individual. I have already claimed the right to speak in terms of 'perspectives' in connection with the imaginative reflection of the self. And we can surely also talk here of the community's perspective on the person. It is not merely that the other members of the community observe the individual, view him or her, and that these perspectives usually converge. (We see the man cross the street, I from here, you from there; but we both see the man cross the street.) It is also the case that the clashes with which we are here concerned are inherently perspectival; or, otherwise put, they are always collisions of interpretations. We have already noted that when, knowing we are speaking of a (whole) person, we say, 'I see him (or her) as X', we announce an interpretation. It matters not whether the person is oneself or another. The earlier remarked limitations on our use of that expression make it clear that persons always are for us objects of, subject to, interpretation. Now wherever there is what we might call a 'standard' interpretation, we may speak of this as the community's perspective. Again, it is not exactly because of a vote of the majority that a particular interpretation is the standard; its commonness is essential, but this commonness is both a result of and an influence on the conduct of the community.

Attributions of self-deception or bad faith will be made, then, when an individual's self-interpretation is thought to disagree with a standard.[1] Someone who is an other to the individual may take himself to speak from the community's perspective, or the individual himself may at some time change perspectives, move to what he lately takes to be the community perspective, and stand to survey his earlier behavior, attitudes, etc. and to assess his earlier interpretation. If this idea of disagreement is to account for attributions of self-deception, we must remember that the imaginative interpretation is not divorced from behavior. The way an individual sees himself – what he sees himself as – can be expressed in his conduct. Neither the fact that someone has made an interpretation of himself – or of some features or stretch of his life – nor the particular tendency or shape of that interpretation is necessarily inaccessible to others.

Of course an individual's self-interpretations may not be obvious either. But that is not a problem for this account. On the contrary, that squares perfectly with the occasional nature of our reasoned attributions of self-deception. As we have remarked, we do not want to call self-deceived everyone who holds inconsistent beliefs about himself and his relations to the world, even if we find these inconsistencies simple to discern; and we do not want to call self-deceived everyone who is not lucid about himself, or who is unaware of some of his relations to or engagements with the world, even if these relations and engagements are ones we think obvious. We assume differences in temperamental endowment or development, and we must recognize the always sporadic character of self-awareness. It is in fact only when it seems clear that there has been self-reflection, and that this self-reflection has yielded an interpretation we take to be clearly at odds with what we expect would be seen through the community's perspective, that we would make the charge of self-deception. This means that there is something overt, there is something about the conduct of the individual we call self-deceived, that is not in harmony with what we feel are socially justified expectations or judgments of him or her. The struggle between the individual's and the community's interpretations is, then, openly waged in social interactions.

This, by the way, begins to explain, indeed reinforces, the intuition that the fragmentariness of imaginative self-reflection is a factor in, that it contributes to, self-deception, though fragmentation is not itself at the core of the puzzle of self-deception. We have not shown the individual in possession of an organized interpretation of his or her whole self, and the community surely need not have a unified picture of the whole person. The dissonance between individual and community can be harsh even if it is sounded only in limited ranges of that human life. What will provide a harmonious resolution for or of the individual and the community will always be a function of the specific discord. Unification or solidification of all the individual's self-interpretations is not the aim and it may not be in the least ameliorative. Nonetheless, it is true that if the individual were for himself or herself in reflection only one object, and if the community, too, could regard each person as only one thing, then it would be much easier to bring into line the individual's and the community's perspectives, to work congruence of those two objects. But it is in fact not easy. The idea that the self depends on imagination grants the complexity of persons and thus both acknowledges and helps to account for the difficulty and the instability of individual and community alignment.

We should also note that the peculiar willfulness of self-deception is not lost in this description. It says that if we ascribe self-deception to someone, we suppose ourselves to be speaking with the power of the community, from a perspective formed by and available to all; we see the object of our ascription asserting an interpretation at odds with the vision of that perspective. There must be, remember, conduct expressive of the fact and the features of the individual's interpretation or we would not take this sort of notice, the notice which leads to our charge. The individual then looks to us willful at every level – in that intentional conduct and in the initial option of, for, his or her singular interpretation.

The emotional tension in the accusation of self-deception must be fully noted. One further source of our sense of the perversity of the self-deceiver may be the fact that an individual's self-interpretations can be variably congenial, variously repellant. The self of imagination may not be a unified object, but some organization prevails in the relative importance and the particular interdependencies of an individual's self-interpretations.[2] (I may see myself as gullible and as trustworthy. The picture of myself as gullible may be of little moment to me, scarcely influencing my thoughts or behavior, easily abandoned as a self-image. The picture of my trustworthiness, on the other hand, may be central to my feelings of identity, extremely important as a stable motivation, a self-image I would be reluctant to forsake, and one tied to other aspects of myself. It may also be, for example, a fount of sustaining pride.) The reactive emotional currents which run through this loose and shifting focal arrangement both add to its complexity and fund some of its driving force. (If I view myself as trusting, and this view is central to my self-conception, the conduct which proceeds from this interpretation will yet vary enormously depending upon whether I am disgusted or delighted by this aspect of myself.) The fact that both the arrangements of and the reactions to self-interpretations will be expressed in behavior then suggests yet another range of opportunities for divergence between the individual and the community. (I see myself first and foremost as a truth-teller; my personal honesty – of which I am proud – impels me to give him certain bad news, painful as it is for him to hear. The community says I am self-deceived about my motive and character. They see me as malicious, and think I should feel ashamed.)

Something like the mosaic analogy can thus be restored: the reservation remains that a whole is never actually completed; not all possible perspectives on an individual will be realized. And the pieces of the mosaic – distinct interpretations, aspects of the self – are never truly cemented in place. The pieces, moreover, are not arranged, even temporarily, on a planar surface. But we now have both the individual and the community presenting accounts of the representation they take this complex and unfinished mosaic to be – and offering something like their aesthetic or moral reactions to the representation they descry – so the prospects for disagreements are clear. But when the community converges on one view, however difficult this object of sight may now seem, if the individual's interpretation does not agree, he or she may be scorned: the individual's waywardness is displayed. And the willfulness we ascribe to self-deception is once again captured.

Even the depth of the feeling that the self-deceiver is one who hides the truth from himself – a seemingly impossible feat – is measured by this account. Calling up as an example Wittgenstein's duck-rabbit, Stanley Cavell remarks:

> We may say that the rabbit-aspect is hidden from us when we fail to see it, the way faces are hidden in drawings of trees. What hides it is obviously not the picture (that reveals it), but our (prior) way of taking it, namely in its duck-aspect. What hides one aspect is another aspect, something at the same level.[3]

And one self-interpretation can obscure another. We say the self-deceiver is hiding the truth from himself when we think the true pattern is so pre-eminently there to be seen. The construction of a different interpretation then looks so artful, as if deliberately fashioned to break or cover our standard. But the self-deceiver is not one who both knows and yet does not know the truth, who must know in order not to know, to hide, to have the truth hidden.

If we see a man's actions as rash and self-serving, and he sees the same actions as courageous and principled, he might know of our interpretation and might even concede that it is not completely inapt, not utterly incompetent: he might say it would fit some cases somewhat like his. But in *this* case he just can't see it.

It might be claimed that the employment in this context of Cavell's remark on the duck-rabbit is infelicitous because, it might be thought, the community's and the individual's interpretations are not 'at the same level' – the community's perspective is larger and more powerful. Several replies would answer this claim. One could substitute another example for the duck-rabbit, in order to model the difference between the individual and the community, and still preserve the point of the remark. Something like a Rorschach ink-blot would provide a good enough comparison. There is a standard interpretation (or perhaps a set of them); it is the standard only as it is the most common response, but there is some power in this commonness: if an individual's response is sufficiently and significantly different from the common interpretation, he or she may be regarded as a deviant and may be treated in a correspondingly special manner. Nevertheless, the ink-blot bears both the common and the idiosyncratic projections, though not together. The blot hides nothing, hides no possibilities, but the viewer takes it as he or she does – brings some elements to the fore and disregards others – and finds, realizes, just one possibility. Thus with another example we reach the same conclusion: one interpretation obscures another.

We might not have bothered with a different illustration, however. One could insist that the difference between the individual and community perspectives does not need modelling, not, anyway, to make this point, because their interpretations already are, in the relevant sense, 'at the same level'. They are, or they are supposed to be, both founded on the same ground. We must assume that both the community and the individual views are directed on the same thing – on a person engaged in just this behavior, expressing just these attitudes, etc. – or else we do not strike a true conflict. If one of the two parties – either the individual or the representative of the community – is ignorant of, radically inattentive to or uninterested in, features of the individual on which an interpretation is based; then there may be no agreement in views, but only because there are not really two views. And there must be two to provoke the clash which sounds the change of self-deception. One may see as foreground what the other sees as background, but they are both looking at the same picture plane, looking 'at the same level'.

There is yet another way of insisting that the individual's and the community's interpretations are at the same level, and this way winds through more difficult terrain, past hard questions about truth and objectivity. Suppose one wants to emphasize that they are at the same level in order to cast doubt on what seems the pre-eminence of the community's view, to unsettle even the idea that one – one or the other – of these interpretations must be more accurate, be correct. Mead's pragmatic account of objectivity ties judgments of objectivity to the usefulness of shared results and the encompassing power of the organization of perspectives. But the interactions between the individual and the community may permit no final judgment of the person, for the relation between them is unceasingly dynamic. If the points along which each of them draws its perspective are constantly transfigured, there may be no point which counts, even provisionally, as objective. There may be nothing worth calling the fact of the matter. To see where, indeed whether, it might be worthwhile to challenge the rule of truth in this sphere, we must study some examples of self-deception.

The cases drawn by Sartre in the second chapter of *Being and Nothingness* will serve well. Let us consider first the waiter, the waiter who

> is quick and forward, a little too precise, a little too rapid. . . .
> He bends forward too eagerly; his voice, his eyes express an interest a little too solicitous for the order of the customer. . . .
> He applies himself to chaining his movements as if they were mechanisms . . .; he gives himself the quickness and pitiless rapidity of things. He is playing. . . . But what is he playing?
> . . . he is playing at being a waiter in a café.[4]

Some features of Sartre's condemnation of this man can be translated into terms close to those of our discussion: the man is in bad faith because he is allowing himself, seeking, to be dominated by the perspective of others. The community sees him as a waiter, and he is committing himself to be the object of their sight and expectations. This for Sartre constitutes bad faith because, in sustaining this role, the man acknowledges his transcendence of it. He has to work so assiduously at being that object because he is not that object. His effort in being that object is proof and an acknowledgment of his subjectivity.

Now if we think the claim that the self is characterized by its being an object to itself is just a neutral description and if we want to maintain that the charge of self-deception, or bad faith, indicates some open conflict between an individual's view and the perspective of the community, then we certainly cannot adopt Sartre's analysis of this case. But if we accept the illustration as a depiction of bad faith, how are we to explain it?

The fact that the job, being a waiter, is a socially-defined role could be, in quite a different way, a part of this man's problem. To say that the community defines what a waiter is, that it has a clear view of what it is to be this 'object', is to suggest that this object is specifically delimited. And if it is thus circumscribed, it is evident that it does not spread over the field of human – even of social – possibilities. Not only are there alternatives – grocer, tailor, auctioneer, etc. – presumably equally well- (and socially-) defined, but there are also other compatible roles – husband, father, son, volunteer fireman, Sunday fisherman – more or less well-defined. The community apparently does not see any human being as all and only a waiter. If the man's behavior discloses his view of himself as the complete waiter, as waiter through and through, all and only waiter, then his interpretation of himself is *not* the one found in the social perspective; and *this* could be the conflict of self-deception. If there could be a society which did insist that being a waiter would exhaust an individual's possibilities – that a waiter cannot now also be other things and, moreover, could never have been anything else – then the members of that society would surely not see Sartre's waiter as a man of bad faith. Their perspectives would converge. And we should not say that the waiter in that community is self-deceived; from our perspective he is socially-deceived.

What should we say of Sartre's woman 'out with a particular man for the first time'? He says the following:

> She knows very well the intentions which the man who is
> speaking to her cherishes regarding her. She knows also that it
> will be necessary sooner or later for her to make a decision. But

she does not want to realize the urgency; she concerns herself only with what is respectful and discreet in the attitude of her companion. She does not apprehend this conduct as an attempt to achieve what we call 'the first approach;' . . . she does not wish to read in the phrases which he addresses to her anything other than their explicit meaning. If he says to her, 'I find you so attractive!' she disarms this phrase of its sexual background. . . . She is profoundly aware of the desire which she inspires, but the desire cruel and naked would humiliate and horrify her. Yet she would find no charm in a respect which would only be respect. . . . [S]uppose he takes her hand. This act of her companion risks changing the situation by calling for an immediate decision. To leave the hand there is to consent in herself to flirt, to engage herself. To withdraw it is to break the troubled and unstable harmony which gives the hour its charm. . . . [T]he young woman leaves her hand there, but she *does not notice* that she is leaving it. She does not notice because it happens by chance that she is at this moment all intellect.[5]

Sartre says this woman is in bad faith and, as he describes her, we should undoubtedly agree. We might try to outline the problem in the pattern of our own analysis, but we could begin only the barest sketch before we would be drawn back to some difficulties with his text. Should we say that the woman sees herself as intellect or as body and soul; while in the community's perspective she is all body, all and only an object which is an object of what might be called 'purely physical' desire? That cannot be right. The community's vision is not so clear, so focused, is it? There is no well-defined role for the 'woman out with a particular man for the first time' as there is for the waiter. The options and limits of her position are not, or are not as clearly, given by widely-shared social definitions. If we want to maintain that she is cast in a role, we might still draw a distinction between merely social and fully personal roles, showing that the latter are not antecedently defined.

But if her situation is really not entirely clear, then how can she *know* all Sartre says she does know? She supposedly knows the man's intentions, that a decision will have to be made, that she is one who must make it. Even at the risk of controverting his larger pieces of doctrine, Sartre insists on the plain objectivity of this situation: there *is* a sexual background to the man's remarks; the man *has* certain intentions; these intentions set a *fixed* course; this conduct *is* an attempt at 'the first approach'; there *is* here 'crucial and naked' desire; to leave the hand *is* to consent to flirt. But do we think this interaction is thus determined? Suppose the man *does* approach this meeting having 'cherished certain intentions'. But seeing this woman now, in this new context, he is no longer moved. Or, in the course of their conversation, she says something he finds deeply offensive. Or, he suddenly remembers and is overwhelmed by a problem with his work. Or who knows what. In recognizing these as – accepting that there are – possibilities, one risks being charged with the turn of mind called in this woman 'self-deceptive'. But if this is what she is thinking, is she definitely wrong?

Herbert Fingarette takes up this example, and his description is even less guarded than Sartre's:

> The hour is entered with flirtatious designs; but the woman disavows any such designs. . . . [S]he manoeuvers her hand with perfect control in such a way as to make it enticingly accessible while refraining from any explicit sexual overture. . . .[6]

From whose or what perspective are *these* actions depicted? Trying for objectivity, we might say that the woman's hand is on the table and we might hesitate to decide whether or not she is presently aware of that fact, but for Fingarette her hand has been made 'enticingly accessible'. He says:

> We should note, for the sake of completeness, that the flirtatious young woman also adopts a self-defensive role: she is the 'intellectual conversationalist'. Of course she disavows this role; just as she carries on her amorous invitations without reflecting upon it, so she carries on the role of 'intellectual' but refuses to reflect upon it. She skilfully presses the conversation in the direction of 'lofty' topics of conversation. But we may assume that, unless she is exceptionally skilful in this role, there will be a certain artificiality, a certain glib irrelevance about her conversation.[7]

To Fingarette the facts are apparent: the young woman *is* flirtatious; she is an *artificial* intellectual. The idea that there must be a fact (or set of facts) of this matter is assumed without question. This seems to me to be a mistake.

But let us suppose what we earlier denied: that an interpretation of 'the woman out with a particular man for the first time' does dominate, has solidified in, the community. Such a woman *is*, in the community's view, the object of physical desire. Then Sartre's young woman, in this community, and inhabiting this role, and yet seeing herself as all intellect, refusing to see what the community sees, will certainly be accused of self-deception. Our analysis explains this charge of self-deception. But it does not commit us to the idea that the community is right in its view, that what the woman is refusing to see is the truth.

Nor, of course, are we committed to the idea that what the woman sees is the truth. But we might yet be divided in our united rejection of both the community's and her views. If one has a conception of persons such that they could never be either just the objects of physical desire or completely intellect, then one could reject both the community's and the woman's perspectives on this ground alone. One could agree that the numbers sharing a given view do not decide its correctness, but still insist that there *is* a correct view, a fact of the matter.

It is easiest to cleave to this position when the region in dispute is one commonly the topic of general theories. But if we begin to carve up this area of contention, to attend to the particular skirmishes, then a general theory – here, of the person – will seem a useless shield, a fortification of objectivity quite beside these issues. From what general theory of intention, for example, can we draw the one true picture of *this* man's intentions at *this* moment? Why must we insist, what is the virtue in the idea, that there *is* such a picture? If we admit that the situation is dynamic, that the course of this hour changes as there is interaction, then only an animated reading should make sense, a constant revision at each instant coloring both the past and the future out of the moving present.

Sartre himself refers to 'the troubled and unstable harmony which gives the hour its charm.' This conception – of an unstable harmony – seems to me to be more powerful here than the assumption of a solid and static truth. What we might in another sphere call 'the truth' may or may not be attractive; but what is fascinating here is the possibility of harmony, the possibility that interpretations which are mutually satisfying can be worked out. Social interactions seem directed by a drive toward satisfaction, not truth – unless, within this realm, one follows James and equates the true with the satisfying. One might recall the pragmatists' suspicion of the fact/value distinction, as in this area the point of the separation of epistemology and ethics is lost. James' wider claim can be scaled down to our topic: he admits that some

> objects of daily use . . . have properties of such constant unwavering importance, and have such stereotyped names, that we end by believing that to conceive them in those ways is to conceive them in the only true way. Those are no truer ways of conceiving them than any others; they are only more important ways, more frequently serviceable ways.*

> *Only if one of our purposes were itself truer than another, could one of our conceptions become the truer conception. To be a truer purpose, however, our purpose must conform more to some absolute standard of purpose in things to which our purposes ought to conform. . . . The only real truth . . ., apart from particular purposes, is the *total* truth.[8]

But people are not these 'objects of daily use'. And the particular position of the specific others in our lives is not 'constant' and 'unwavering', 'stereotyped'. How can we hold to the idea of the one true conception of a given person? Should we not always expect to have to search for the 'important' and the 'serviceable' interpretations? Would it not be presumptuous to think ourselves devoid of particular purposes – or to think ourselves to have only the one true purpose – in any social interchange? Such a thought could anyway never be sustained under the endorsed account of the self, because this account tells us that we (and our purposes) are not immediately transparent to ourselves: we must try to achieve or share the viewpoint of another, and we have no guarantee of success.

And it still seems that success will always be a matter, or a promise, of social harmony. Discord need not, however, be equated with a failure to grasp the other's interpretation. But if one grasps and flatly rejects it, and if one is not at all moved to modify one's own perspective, then the other's view is obviously unappealing – that is, it seems to one to offer, to prepare for, no satisfaction, no shared satisfaction. Some social relations are maintained in these circumstances, without the prospect of sympathy. Think of Sartre's young woman in that community with its rigid view of her as an object of physical desire. She may not be oblivious to the community's perspective, and she might, with this man, feel that construal now in place. She might even realize that the picture is not radically inappropriate or utterly unfitting. But if it is not the picture on which she has pinned her hopes, she may set about its destruction, trying to refute it in word, deed, mien.[9] Such a wholly deadly mission surely carries no possibility of mutual satisfaction. It is not merely that its aim is the annihilation of the other's view; there is the additional problem that, with that annihilation, the woman's project is dissipated. If all her efforts have been strategic to demolition, then there has been no conservation, and certainly no promotion, of whatever self-interpretation she might have originally had. If she has been consumed in the activity of destroying an image, then she has not rested content in the possession of one.

But, happily, our social interactions are not usually so catastrophic. We expect to undergo mutual influence, not liquidation. Indeed, we may gravitate to a pool of companions who will reinforce, or at least not destructively erode, our self-interpretations. Then, even if we are out of line from the larger community's perspective, we may preserve ourselves in this smaller community and perhaps enlist their support, or join with them in a political struggle, to see the minority perspective prevail. (So, for example, Sartre's unfortunate young woman could have a sister who is an active feminist, someone working and loving confidently, contending vigorously, with others, for a more egalitarian vision. This sister would have, and would continue to build, her community.)

In fact, most people must feel that they are typically in tune with, or are clearly anticipating what should, what must become, the perspective of the community; and that may help explain the ease which many feel in attributing self-deception to specific others. That, together with the actual need for individual adjustment within the living and developing community and the fact that human beings bear, invite, various interpretations, is enough to account for the frequency of the feeling of particular conflict which is vented in the charge of self-deception.

SELF-KNOWLEDGE

If some of the puzzles of self-deception can be pieced together by focusing on the divergence of individual and community perspectives, perhaps we can find clues to self-knowledge by attending to the convergence of these perspectives. Some might be ill-disposed toward a search which begins here, for it might seem that self-knowledge has, essentially, nothing to do with others: it demands introspection, a good and clear look inward, and I am always in a better position to do this than anyone else; I, in fact, occupy the only proper position, the only position which allows a view. Others do not have a perspective on this, so I need not look for convergence.

But, of course, if we accept the idea that the self is a social object, then the disposition to equate knowing the self with introspecting is dispersed. Settling on the claim that the self is produced as an object in imagination, however, we may seem again to approach the belief that it will be known only in solitude. But then we will remember that imagination, too, is tied to the social community and that we find that the imaginative apprehension of the self can be produced by, show itself in, have effects on, the conduct of the individual and the others.

However, even if we do keep before us the ideas of the self and imagination which have been presented, and even if they remain attractive, there can seem obstacles to accepting a notion of self-knowledge explicated in terms of the convergence of one's own and the community's perspectives. In particular, what eventually seemed stepping stones to an understanding of self-deception may reappear here as boulders blocking this path to a view of self-knowledge. We earlier suggested that a community's interpretations might not, despite their coercive power, be right; that, in fact, there may be no one right interpretation of a person, no one given fact of this matter. But if we have been cut loose from the moorings of facts and correctness, how can we ever secure a concept of knowledge?

I do not think safe harbor for the concept of self-knowledge must be found in the shelter of facts. If we have denied that the community's view is necessarily *right*, we have not denied the force of the community in the *validation* of an interpretation. And if we navigate carefully with this idea of validation we may yet reach, if not the solid ground of certainty, at least an adequately fortified and comfortable bay.

That a claim to some personal characteristics requires, and requires nothing more than, social validation is obvious but sometimes forgotten: we surely cannot alone judge whether we are, for example, charming, unattractive, insolent, vulgar. And if we may begin to wish for, and conceive of, a court beyond our community to consider whether we are, for instance, intelligent, foolish, courageous, tedious, we still feel, and grant, the force of social validation. There may be many traits or features which we sometimes do feel we alone are in a, or in the best, position to discern and fairly judge in ourselves – say, honesty, innocence, discontent, devotion. If there is anything which sustains such feelings it must be a sense that others do not know our full story, that they have not been attentive or careful or constant in their observation, or that our powers have not been fully disclosed, that we have not been properly tried or have not faced the right tests or found the right opportunities. Because we must admit that even these characteristics are tested, tried, and expressed in the right opportunities. This is in their very natures; and it is, for example, only a tested honesty which allows one the claim to honesty. If we remember all this, we should be less inclined to doubt the length of the community's reach or the firmness of the grasp which holds only our conduct. And if we see it has this much power, we need not look beneath the floor of the community's shared judgments to find a sure prop for our own self-assessments. Then, if we do disagree with others in our pictures of ourselves, we still need no deeper foundation on which to make our stand than a sense of the conduct which, if displayed or if finally attended to, would convince them, secure agreement.

Accepting these constraints on self-ascriptions, accepting the idea of community validation of claims to self-knowledge, we lose the immediacy as well as the certainty of those claims. But if one has ever felt uncertain about one's self, has ever been surprised by oneself, or has once admitted another's superior insight about a region of one's self, then the loss is a gain. Now, however, if self-knowledge is not something one just immediately has, then one must expect to expend effort in its acquisition.

I want to suggest that the ongoing enterprise of the production of images – or pictures or interpretations – of the self is the mirror of the activity of self-knowledge. That is to say, it reflects the fact that self-knowledge *is* an activity; the self is not a fixed and complete entity and knowledge of it is not fixed or achieved once and for all. My suggestion also carries the claim that the production of these interpretations requires self-knowledge. They are the images of self-knowledge. This suggests, then, given our earlier discussion of the self, that having a self is inextricably bound with knowing that self. This does not cross the assertion that self-knowledge is not something one just has, for we have seen that the self is not something one just has. It must develop and be possessed.

We may, then, with this suggestion, mark one small portion of a larger claim: that the self is that to which one is fated to stand in the relations which one may or may not bear to others:

> . . . any other is one whom I may just not know, have no relation with; but I cannot just not know, or have no relation with, myself. Ignorance of myself is something I must work at; it is something studied, like a dead language.[10]

If we believe that the existence of the self depends on the exercise of imagination, then insofar as one has a self, one is making some interpretation of the self.[11] If one is in possession of a self, then one has made some construal. One might work at ignorance of it. But if ignorance 'is something studied, like a dead language'; then knowledge is something that naturally develops. And I think it develops through interactions with others, as does one's native language.

We earlier described a man who suddenly, in reflection after a reunion, sees himself as his family's peacemaker. But he might have been a person who does what he does at the family reunions because, antecedently, he sees himself as the peacemaker. And he might have been cast in this role by others, through their treatment of him and out of their needs; or he might have cast himself, out of his own needs. There is extreme difficulty in any attempt to disentangle the elements of the self thrown upon it from the elements it has actively sought. The fusion of these makes the very glass of the self-image, as every interpretation mirrors in its own structure this same pattern of passivity and activity. One both makes and suffers one's self-interpretations.[12] One both constructs and yet learns from them; one can be surprised by them. The imagination here is not just a toy with which we illustrate the intellect; it is itself cognitive. And it is affective. One is moved by what one sees. As the self is given in imagination one actually explores or reforms one's position and relations to others and the environment. And, as one then behaves from a sense of that position or stands to preserve those relations, one meets the reactions of others.

Here the conformation of activity and passivity is presented again, as one must work to grasp the views and take the viewpoints of the others and, then, let their responses make an impression and finally see their sights. Then, when one's perspective on oneself converges with the perspective of the community, one will feel self-knowledge secured. Again, it seems all one can try for is an interpretation which works. If the community is not satisfied, it will continue to make its demands. In extreme straits, the individual may seek or work toward, appeal to, a different community, a community of another time or place. But even in ordinary circumstances of discord, the individual can modify as well as answer the reigning demands. Of course the individual, too, is modified in social adjustment. But if it is unclear whether social interaction produces a change in the self or in self-perception, that is because, again, these are inextricably bound. A self which comes to see itself differently is a different self.

SELF-INTEREST AND EGOCENTRICITY

There is one last moral I should like to draw from this story of the self. It concerns the nature of self-interest and the practical problem of egocentricity. We have insisted both that the possession of the self requires something like taking the attitude of an other, becoming an object to oneself, and that connection with this object–self is effected through imagination. But surely imagination can also link us to others. Indeed it does so in the very act of self-reflection: for if one apprehends oneself imaginatively as another does, as an object, one is also assuming the subjectivity of the other. This does not mean, of course, that one actually achieves the particular attitude of a particular other. But it does begin to discredit some claims for the metaphysical priority of egocentricity, for it shows that recognition of self requires recognition of others. And it suggests that the mode through which we might fasten to others and their interests is the very mode through which we are attached to ourselves.

William Hazlitt, in 'An Essay on the Principles of Human Action', presents a relevant argument. He wants to show that

> the human mind is naturally disinterested, or that it is naturally interested in the welfare of others in the same way and from the same direct motives, by which we are impelled on the pursuit of our own interest.[13]

Hazlitt says he must admit that each of us has a 'mechanical' interest in his or her own past and present: there is a direct and exclusive connection wrought of memories and sensations. But the present and the past are not modified by efforts of the will; voluntary interests are pursued only into the future. 'It is only from the interest excited in him by future objects that man becomes a moral agent, or is denominated selfish, or the contrary, according to the manner in which he is affected by what relates to his own *future* interest, or that of others' (*CW*, p. 385). And an individual has no exclusive mechanical connection with future objects. They are given only in imagination.

> The imagination, by means of which alone I can anticipate future objects, or be interested in them, must carry me out of myself to the feelings of others by one and the same process by which I am thrown forward as it were into my future being, and interested in it. I could not love myself, if I were not capable of loving others. Self-love, used in this sense, is in its fundamental principle the same with disinterested benevolence (*CW*, p. 385).

Hazlitt is directing his remarks against those who believe that human beings are naturally selfish, that self-interest is the first motive for and a fundamental principle of human action. One who holds this belief need not, of course, insist that there are never unselfish acts: moral instruction and/or training in other habits of action might effectively control the natural propensity to further only one's own good. Or it could be that, as each individual is dependent on others, individual self-seeking must encompass some concern for the welfare of these others. The dispute is not, then, centered on a calculation of the frequency of selfishness in society. It is rather a question of the origin of both selfish and unselfish action. Hazlitt is denying the primacy of selfishness, and thus denying that it must be either overcome through instruction or training or allied to a circle of interdependent beings.

We would have to step beside the course of our proceedings to examine in detail Hazlitt's notion of personal identity and his views on voluntary action. The shortest summary would better place his thoughts in our path. He says that we might well regard an individual as a set of sections – his or her life might span a variety of selves.[14] The present self and the past – or aspects of them – can be connected by a consciousness which does not in the same way reach to the present and past of others. But the future is not separately parcelled out, and the connection one makes with one's future self can equally be made to the futures of others.

> Suppose a number of men employed to cast a mound into the sea. As far as it has gone, the workmen pass backwards and forwards on it, it stands firm in its place, and though it recedes farther and farther from the shore, it is still joined to it. A man's personal identity and self-interest have just the same principle and extent, and can reach no farther than his actual existence. But if a man of a metaphysical turn, seeing that the pier was not yet finished, but was to be continued to a certain point and in a certain direction, should take it into his head to insist that what was already built and what was to be built were the same pier, that the one must afford as good footing as the other, and should accordingly walk over the pier-head on the solid foundation of his metaphysical hypothesis – he would argue . . . not a whit more absurdly than those who found a principle of absolute self-interest on a man's future identity with his present being. But say you, the comparison does not hold in this, that the man *can* extend his thoughts . . . beyond the present moment, whereas in the other case he cannot move a single step forwards. Grant it. This will only shew that the mind has wings as well as feet, which of itself is a sufficient answer to the selfish hypothesis (*CW*, p. 424).

He declares that all voluntary action must have as its impulse an idea presented by the imagination, for we move 'from the will' to produce or prevent foreseen but yet non-existent consequences. This idea, this object of imagination, is an object with a specific nature, and that nature is not a function of the object's connection with any particular person. The idea of a burn, for example, is the idea of something painful, and pain is pain no matter who feels it. If one shrinks from fire, anticipating a burn, it is not because of a thought of one's self, but because of a thought of pain. And there must be, in general, 'something in the very idea of good, or evil, which naturally excites desire or aversion, which is in itself the proper motive of action, which impels the mind to pursue the one and to avoid the other' (*CW*, p. 396). If this were not so, Hazlitt contends, we could never even develop self-interest. We would be complacent, unmoved, neither seeking nor avoiding anything. But with the foresight of imagination and the natural desire for happiness, we can behave partially, attracted to and seeking this or repelled by and avoiding that.

Self-love can thus be deduced, Hazlitt asserts, from the imaginative capacity and the objective nature of good and evil. One does not simply love oneself because one is oneself. '[O]r shall we suppose that a man's attachment to himself is because he has a long nose or a short one, because his hair is black or red, or from an unaccountable fancy for his own name . . .?' (*CW*, p. 406).

Hazlitt's idea is that self-love is, in its origin, 'an impersonal feeling' (*CW*, p. 396). It is engendered by facts of the world and human capacities which are as readily directed into benevolence toward others. Anything which can be an object of imagination can be an object of interest; it is the good – not one's good, but the good – which moves one; the lives of others can be imagined; therefore, one can be interested in, desire and seek, the good for those others.

Appealing as they are, Hazlitt's convictions do not accord in all details with conclusions which would be drawn from our remarks on the self. We could not close the curtain as he does on the present and the past, assured that 'all voluntary action must relate solely to the future' (*CW*, p. 424). Of course the past cannot be undone, but the patterns it presents can be altered, the patterns one sees may change, and it is just these patterns which may interest the self. Present and future actions may be required if an individual is to secure one interpretation of his or her past, rather than another, but what the individual counts on in performing those acts is their relation to the past. Hazlitt wants to reject the idea that the past can provide an impulse to voluntary action because, as he grants that each has the exclusive, 'mechanical' attachment of memory only to his or her own past, he would otherwise feel obliged to admit that human action might be naturally directed by concerns wrapped tightly about the self.

We, however, need not share his worry, his sense that 'the selfish hypothesis' must be turned back by a wall which would set off and seal in the present and past. He himself would not mind breaking down this barrier once he noticed that the present and the past enter as the objects of willfully self-interested action through the door of imagination. It is as one is working out of or seeking to confirm in or from the present or past a particular interpretation of the self that these voluntary actions may be said to be related to, directed by, the present or past. But the interpretation is the product of the imagination, so the engine of the self-interested propulsive force of the present or past is, finally, imagination, and not those 'mechanisms' of memory and sensation. With this view Hazlitt would once again feel his thesis safe. The foundation for interested action is re-established on imagination, and Hazlitt maintains that this ties an individual to another's interests as well as to his or her own.

But it is just this central claim which Hazlitt never secures. He simply assumes the existence of sympathetic imagination, vouching for a 'natural disposition of the mind to sympathize with the feelings of others' (*CW*, p. 398), taking the burden of his argument to be confined to the demonstration that we are interested in our own welfare only through 'the faculty by which [we are] originally interested in the welfare of others' (*CW*, p. 401). One might contend that he offers, in the whole corpus of his criticism, a pragmatic justification for this assumption, as he often relies on this notion of sympathetic imagination and so draws out and considers the consequences of his conception. And we must admit that his doctrine of sympathetic identification seems plainly plausible when our attention is limited to the future: all we can do is imagine the future, not really feel it; if Hazlitt tells us we can imagine it *with* others, along lines which place these others as the points of origin, this imposes very little on the sense we may cherish of our own originality and of the separateness of our actual feelings.

But if my account of the self will not sustain that limitation to the future, if it takes us back as well to an interest in the past and the present, it also contains the vehicle to carry us out of any necessity of self-centeredness. It claims that to have a self and hence, of course, to have any self-interest, one must assume the viewpoint or attitude of another. As this is done through imagination, there is – this is – sympathetic imagination; for it involves the idea that another *has* an attitude and that one is sharing it. And this idea is rightly called 'sympathy'.

If sympathy forms the basis of the sense of self, then we do not face an inevitable, or inescapable because ontological, problem or task of empathy. Empathy requires the projection of the self into another. The concept of empathy is a fairly recent discovery (or invention), called in to serve some aesthetic theories; and we can see why it was readily enlisted in descriptions of the active contemplation of inanimate objects. The idea of empathy seems founded on the supposition that the object of empathy is not already full, as it were, or saturated with its own feelings. One can yet pour in one's self. On the understanding of the self we have been exploring, however, one has nothing to project, nothing to pour, unless one has antecedently granted the attitudes, viewpoints, perspectives of others. Then these others may seem from the start too full or too distant to allow empathy.

What they and we both may need is more sympathy. And if we fail to sympathize appropriately, this should count as an intellectual and emotional, a moral, a practical failure. It is not an inadequacy to which our evolution leaves us the natural heirs. The idea that selfishness is a biological legacy may be the most potent contemporary version of a problem or excuse formerly offered a priori. Representative, but particularly telling, is a plain statement of this idea by Derek Parfit.

Although Parfit wants to argue that self-interest is not the foundation for rational behavior, that a special concern for one's own future is not rationally justified, he thinks we all do *have* such a feeling of interest and special concern. This ubiquity is not a justification, not even so much as a reason to think the attitude justified, however, because, he claims, this special concern has an evolutionary explanation:

Special concern for one's own future would be selected by evolution. Animals without such concern would be more likely to die before passing on their genes. Such concern would remain, as a natural fact, even if we decided it was not justified.[15]

But if we take an impartial survey of the living world, at the level of its biology, of the animals and plants in nature, the nature of which we are a part; can we find or make sense of success stories which hinge on the plot device of a 'special concern for one's own future'? Was the Mesozoic hegemony of the reptiles in any way a function of self-interested attitudes? Or did those dinosaurs' extraordinarily long dominion over the animal kingdom finally come to an end because they were insufficiently self-centered? Can the comparative rise in the fortunes of the mammals or the pervasive establishment and the irrepressible prosperity of the insect class be attributed to these animals' self-concern? Is the male black widow spider then anomalously altruistic? He would be inexplicable on this theory of evolution: If he had any 'special concern for [his] own future', he would surely 'die before passing on [his] genes'; for he would not risk mating at all.

The idea that biological evolution selects for self-concern in either the individual or the species (or the gene) is an idea not fit to survive. No mere sport of language, no merely verbal maneuver leads us to the conclusion that self-interest requires some measure of self-possession. And we possess our selves through sharing the perspectives of others. If we then feel some special concern for ourselves, it is not our biology but our social context which has spawned it.

And if we feel some special concern for others, we may try our sympathy. But if we are in fact to sympathize with particular others, then we must in fact share their feelings, grasp or know their attitudes. Hazlitt, while holding that there is no natural inclination to selfishness or innate self-love, is himself struck by the ontogenetic problem, and he feels he must explain what looks like selfishness in the very young child.

He says that the child indeed pursues the good impersonally, not as *his* or *hers* but as *the* good, just as does everyone, except those who have cultivated habits of self-love. The child has not yet in fact had a chance to become truly selfish: this habit requires a firm sense of both self and others, so that one can favor the former over the latter. 'A child is insensible to the good of others not from any want of goodwill towards them, or an exclusive attachment to self, but for want of knowing better' (*CW*, p. 396). The child cannot act first from an attachment to self because he or she may not yet have an idea of self. If he seems to seek his own gratification in preference to the good for others, this is 'because he has a more distinct idea of his own wants and pleasures than of theirs' (*CW*, p. 396). The implication seems to be that once the child comprehends the basic distinction between individuals, realizes his own self, the separateness of himself from others, and their separateness from one another, sympathetic imagination will enable him to move past his own more immediate gratification to take an interest in any individual's. But, still, the child must actually know what others want, what their pleasures are, if he is to act benevolently. And this, Hazlitt suggests, will always be a problem with the pursuit of the good of others:

> I know better what my future feelings will be than what those of others will be in the like case. . . . It is chiefly from this greater readiness and certainty with which we can look forward into our own minds than out of us into those of other men, that that strong and uneasy attachment to self . . . takes its rise . . . (*CW*, p. 426).

But we have seen reason to doubt that certainty is a concept at play in self-knowledge. And what of this 'greater readiness' to look 'into our own minds'? We have seen reason to believe that any reflection on the self must be directed by a thought of others' attitudes. Of course, these may not be the others with whom we are in company. A specific form of self-deception which we might have noted is the construction of others out of one's own attitudes. But the fact is that we can attend to the reactions of particular others, and that our interpretations of our selves and these others can suffer revisions in our interactions. Is there then any reason to deny that we can thus achieve the appropriate access to these others, achieve, that is, a true sympathy?

The epistemic concern simply dissolves into the search for harmony. We may, of course, not always choose to seek harmony; but if we do, the resources of imagination are plumbed. And just as imagination can take us to our selves, it can carry us out of and beyond ourselves – if we are interested, if we see some object as dearer to us than ourselves.

NOTES

INTRODUCTION

1 Gilbert Ryle, *The Concept of Mind* (New York: Barnes & Noble, 1949), p. 245.
2 René Descartes, *Meditation VI*, in *Philosophical Works of Descartes*, trans. Haldane and Ross (New York: Dover, 1955), vol. 1, p. 186.
3 René Descartes, *Meditations II*, trans. Haldane and Ross, vol. 1, p. 152.
4 Descartes, *Reply to Objections V*, trans. Haldane and Ross, vol. 2, p. 231.
5 John B. Watson, *Behaviorism* (New York: W. W. Norton & Company, 1930), p. 3.
6 *Social Psychology*, *Sociological Perspectives*, ed. Morris Rosenberg and Ralph H. Turner (New York: Basic Books, 1981), p. 7.
7 Peter L. Berger, 'Identity as a Problem in the Sociology of Knowledge', in James E. Curtis and John W. Petras (eds) *The Sociology of Knowledge* (New York: Praeger Publishers, 1970), p. 373. Berger's article originally appeared in the *Journal of Sociology*, VII (1966), pp. 105–15.
8 This quotation is from Charles Morris, *The Pragmatic Movement in America* (New York: George Braziller, 1970), p. 187. Dewey's memorial address was originally published under the title 'George Herbert Mead', in the *Journal of Philosophy*, 28 (1931), pp. 309–14.
9 This quotation appears in David L. Miller, *George Herbert Mead, Self, Language, and the World* (Chicago: The University of Chicago Press, 1973), p. ix. It is from a 1938 University of Chicago Press announcement. The phrase Whitehead quotes from Dewey occurs in the latter's

preface to Mead's *The Philosophy of the Present*, edited by Arthur E. Murphy (Chicago: The University of Chicago Press, 1980). (*The Philosophy of the Present* was originally published by Open Court in 1932.)
10 George H. Mead, *Mind, Self, and Society: from the Standpoint of a Social Behaviorist*, edited by Charles W. Morris (Chicago: The University of Chicago Press, 1934), p. 10.
   Hereafter, references to this work will be made by parenthetical notations, using the abbreviations '*MSS*'.
11 Rom Harré, 'Some Remarks on "Rule" as a Scientific Concept', in Theodore Mischel (ed.) *Understanding Other Persons*, (Totowa, New Jersey: Rowman & Littlefield, 1974), p. 147.
12 ibid., p. 166.
13 R. S. Peters, 'Personal Understanding and Personal Relationships', in Theodore Mischel (ed.), *Understanding Other Persons*, p. 42.
14 Basil Bernstein, 'Social Class, Language and Socialization', in Pier Paolo Giglioli (ed.) *Language and Social Context* (New York: Penguin Books, 1972), p. 159. This paper was originally published in Bernstein's *Class, Codes and Control, vol. one: Theoretical Studies Towards A Sociology of Language* (London: Routledge & Kegan Paul, 1970) and as an article in *Current Trends in Linguistics, Vol. 12*, ed. A. S. Abramson *et al.* (The Hague: Mouton Press, 1971).
15 Lionel Trilling, *The Liberal Imagination* (New York: Viking Press, 1950), p. 9.

CHAPTER 1: MEAD'S THEORY OF THE SELF

1 George H. Mead, *Selected Writings*, edited by Andrew J. Reck (Indianapolis: Bobbs-Merrill Company, Inc., 1964), p. 142.
   Hereafter, references to this work will be made by parenthetical notations, using the abbreviation '*SW*'.
2 Perhaps Mead can salvage a variant of his generalization by a restricted use of the word 'behavior'. Although we can speak of the behavior of a mushroom exposed to sunlight, of the behavior of a paramecium immersed in salt water, Mead may want to insist on a more limited sense of the word and consider it equivalent to, say, 'conduct'.
3 The sexist strains of English present insuperable problems for a text such as this. So many sentences will require not just a third-person singular pronoun, but the reflexive form as well as the subjective, objective, and possessive cases, that actually using both (and sometimes all) the appropriate genders would produce prose specimens long and iterated enough to block comprehension. Other devices – the use of the feminine throughout, or some version of equal representation, say alternation – are also often precluded by the requirement that the prose connect sensibly with the prose of Mead

and others, all of whom use the masculine forms almost exclusively. There seems to be no happy solution. I shall enter reminders when I can, and shall certainly myself remember, that at least half the individuals developing and possessing selves are female.

4 This example is proposed by Israel Scheffler in *Four Pragmatists* (London: Routledge & Kegan Paul, 1974), p. 157.
5 Ludwig Wittgenstein, *Philosophical Investigations*, trans. by G. E. M. Anscombe (New York: The Macmillan Company, 1953), p. 192.
  Hereafter, references to this work will be made by parenthetical notation, using the abbreviation '*PI*'.
6 This is not to say that I do *not* ordinarily hear myself when I speak; I do, and if I were suddenly unable to, or did not, hear myself while speaking, I would want some special explanation: I might wonder whether I had become deaf, whether my larynx had somehow been damaged, or whatever. The explanation could, of course, be obvious: if I were speaking in the midst of a din, I would not expect to hear myself. This sort of example in fact, however, supports the general claim of an asymmetry between my relation to my words and another's relation to them. In the din I should shout directly into the other's ear, for he or she would have to hear my voice, as I would not, to know if I were speaking. I do not *have* to hear my own voice to know what I am saying. (There may be some genetic questions which are here not addressed: Can I in the din forgo the sound of my voice only because I have a normal auditory history? And is it only as an adult that my knowledge of what I am saying does not depend on self-audition? The problems faced by deaf children trying to learn to speak might well suggest affirmative answers to such questions; but the issue is complex. Deaf children, after all, not only never hear their own voices; they are also unable to hear others, to hear, in particular, others' attempted corrections of their own sounds. It might be argued that this second sort of deprivation is the more crucial. Pertinent similarities and differences are presented by the cases of children with certain speech impediments. A child with normal hearing ability and a minor speech impediment – a lisp, for example – may well require therapy, directed intervention, despite the fact that he or she could, all alone, listen to his or her own defective speech.)
7 If, following William James, we think 'reality "independent" of human thinking . . . seems a thing very hard to find' (*Pragmatism* (Cambridge: Harvard University Press, 1978), p. 119); if we think that it is 'we [who] break the flux of sensible reality into things' (ibid., p. 122), that not just constellations, but stars, too, are carved out as objects by human selectivity, association, and emphasis; we can, nevertheless, mark with this example a relevant distinction between two sorts of cases. If the groupings which constitute the constellations are not more arbitrary than those which cast the stars in our heavens, they are certainly more complex: they must fold in and reiterate human choices; for if we shape the stars, then constellations are shapings of already shaped material. And it seems that, at some level of

complexity, symbols are both required for and empower continuing selectivity and the elaboration of particular emphases.
8 C. H. Cooley, *Human Nature and the Social Order* (New York: Scribner's, 1902, rev. edn 1922), p. 84.
9 Ibid., p. 85, p. 87.
10 Ibid., p. 134.

CHAPTER 2: IMAGINATION

1 Israel Scheffler argues (in 'Mead on Explanation . . .', *Four Pragmatists*, pp. 170–4) that Mead's distinction between reduction and explanation is confused in both its statement and practice. Mead asserts that a functional interpretation of mind can, without mistaken reduction, explain mental phenomena in terms of non-mental phenomena. But Scheffler points out that a functional explanation which contains only behavioristic terms would, in fact, constitute a complete reduction. If Mead's explanations are allowed to depart from 'purely behavioristic terms' (cf. *MSS*, p. 10), as they in fact do, to construe the mind in terms of 'attitudes', 'dispositions', and 'latencies', then the objection to Watson becomes unclear. Are Watson's 'conditioned reflexes' any more reductionistic than 'attitudes' or 'dispositions'? Are *any* of these observable physical objects or observable properties of physical objects? Furthermore, if Mead is content to retain in his interpretation of mind terms unreduced to the physical or behavioristic, then his insistence on a functional account as the key to explanation is perhaps misguided. The correlation of unreduced mental dispositions with physical phenomena, the delineation of causal relationships between them, does not depend upon functionalism. Such correlations and causal connections could, in the same way, be proposed in explanations of 'psychic entities' of the sort Mead wants to deny (*MSS*, p. 10).

Scheffler is certainly correct in his assessment of and objection to Mead's treatment of explanation. But if we note once again Mead's rather uncommon assumption that imagery functions in behavior, we may yet hold out some hope that his remarks on this limited topic might offer a novel perspective on imagination, a perspective which it would not be inappropriate to call 'behavioristic'.
2 George H. Mead, *Movements of Thought in the Nineteenth Century*, edited by Merritt H. Moore (Chicago: University of Chicago Press, 1936), p. 398.
Hereafter, references to this work will be made by parenthetical notations, using the abbreviation '*MT*'.
3 I will conform to most contemporary discussions of imagination if I cite as representative Hume's remarks in *A Treatise of Human Nature*, edited by L. A. Selby-Bigge (Oxford: Clarendon Press, 1951), Book I, Part I, Sections I and II.

4 Jean-Paul Sartre, *L'Imaginaire* (Paris: Gallimard, 1940), p. 35.
  Hereafter, references to this work will be made by parenthetical notations, using the abbreviation '*I*'.
  References to the Philosophical Library translation, *The Psychology of Imagination* (London: Methuen & Co., 1972) will be made using the abbreviation '*I(e)*'.
  This remark occurs on *I(e)*, p. 14.
5 Cf. *I*, p. 13; *I(e)*, p. 1: 'There have been psychologists . . . who maintained that a vivid image could not be distinguished from a faint perception. . . . But we shall see . . . that such claims rest on an error. In fact, the confusion is impossible; what has come to be known as an "image" occurs immediately as such to reflection.' Or p. 15: 'The classical authors described the image as a faint, vague perception but in all other respects like the perception in the "flesh". Now we know this to be an error.'
6 Descartes thinks the sketch example so persuasive that he employs it to ease Gassendi to acceptance of a different point, viz., that our ideas of a true triangle is not derived from the senses. Descartes asserts that even the best of the triangles we *see* are actually bumpy and irregular, but when we see such a figure drawn on paper, we apprehend not it but our own idea of a triangle.

> This is exactly the same as when we look at a piece of paper on which little strokes have been drawn with ink to represent a man's face; for the idea produced in us in this way is not so much that of the lines of the sketch as of the man. But this could not have happened unless the human face had been known to us by other means . . . (*Reply to Objections V*, trs. Haldane and Ross, vol. two, p. 228).

Descartes thinks it immediately obvious that we don't actually *perceive* the man; the strokes of ink are given to the senses, but *we* put the man there. We *have* to know the face by other means, because it's not given in the seeing of the sketch.
  Ryle's concern with the distinction between seeing a picture and imagining its subject is more direct. Of course, his primary objective is to deny that imagining is the seeing of mental pictures, but he asserts: '. . . having paper pictures before the eyes . . . is a familiar stimulus to imaging.' 'This is what snapshots are for.' Indeed, so strong is Ryle's interest in this 'stimulus to imaging' that he declares: 'I should not keep [a] portrait if it did not perform this function' (*The Concept of Mind*, pp. 253–4).
7 Hume, *A Treatise of Human Nature*, Book I, Part I, Section I.
8 Ibid.
9 A third option, citation of the 'Perky effect', has been available since 1910. C. W. Perky's experiment involved asking subjects seated before an initially blank screen to project onto the screen the visual image of an object, for example, a banana. Hidden from the subjects, an assistant in the next room would then project a very faint picture of

a banana onto the screen. Asked to describe what they had imagined, the subjects usually produced a description which fitted, in detail, the pictured banana. Cf. 'An Experimental Study of Imagination', *American Journal of Psychology* (1910), vol. 23, 422–52.

If we do not choose to be as imperiously dismissive as Sartre – 'One does not know who is more lacking in understanding, the experimenter who asks such questions or the subject who responds to them so submissively' (*I*, p. 109; *I(e)*, p. 60) – we can still insist that these results do not disturb the claim that the phenomenological difference between deliberately producing a mental image of an object and perceiving that object is manifest. Discussion of the Perky experiment in this context is complicated by the fact that what is supposedly confused with a mental image of an object is, after all, not the object itself but another sort of image or picture. But if that complication is put aside, it is still not clear that the Perky experiment shows the confusion of a deliberately produced mental image with a perception. For it is not clear that the subjects have succeeded in producing any mental images. Indeed, their failures to describe anything other than the public picture of, for example, the banana would seem to indicate that they *have* no images of their own to describe.

This is not to beg the question of whether imagination is exercised by the subjects of the Perky experiments, or the larger question of whether imagination and perception can be mixed. One might, in fact, describe the Perky effect as the incorporation of perceived material into an imaginative projection and, thus, assimilate it to such a phenomenon as the seeing of figures in an inkblot. Seeing a face in inkblot #3 may well be regarded as an imaginative act, but it is certainly different from simply imagining a face, purposely calling to mind, in an image, the face of Pierre. The connection between cases of these different sorts will be taken up in the sequel.

10 Sartre's accounts of hallucination and dream can be found on pp. 286–340 *I*, pp. 171–206 *I(e)*.

11 Another moral can also be drawn. With the mention of hallucinations and dreams, the epistemological balance seems redressed. We noted earlier (p. 50) Sartre's advantage in needing neither to describe nor to postulate a mechanism to account for the distinction we can usually so effortlessly make between perceiving and imagining. But if those who assimilate imagining and perceiving face (or ignore) a difficulty with their view at that point, it seems Sartre must face the inverse difficulty. If 'we distinguish immediately between images and perceptions', if we 'recognize immediately that . . . images are images' (*I*, p. 287; *I(e)*, p. 171); how could a man ever ask, 'Is this a dagger which I see before me, The handle toward my hand?'; how could a man declare that 'in the night I dreamt that I found myself in this particular place, that I was dressed and seated near the fire, whilst in reality, I was lying undressed in bed!' declare that 'on many occasions I have in sleep been deceived by . . . illusions' – 'I am now seeing light, hearing a noise, feeling heat. These objects are unreal, for I am asleep; but at

least I seem to see, to hear, to be warmed'? Sartre is not unaware of the special difficulties these cases present to him.

12 In fact, as Israel Scheffler has noted, we may trade upon the similarity when, to encourage a child learning to use our language, we ask him or her to point to a tree, a dog, a flower, for example, not in the park but in a picture book. This use of language, which Scheffler calls 'mention-selective', is obviously not limited to children. Moreover, it can help account for our learning to use terms with null extensions, terms such as 'centaur', 'unicorn', 'chimeral'. Cf. 'Ambiguity: An Inscriptional Approach' in *Logic and Art, Essays in Honor of Nelson Goodman*, edited by R. Rudner and I. Scheffler (Indianapolis: The Bobbs-Merrill Company, Inc., 1972); and *Beyond the Letter* (London: Routledge & Kegan Paul, 1979), especially Chapter I, section 10; II, 4, 7; III, 1.

13 Bernard Williams, 'Imagination and the Self', in *Studies in the Philosophy of Thought and Action*, edited by P. F. Strawson (London: Oxford University Press, 1968), p. 205.

14 Hide Ishiguro, 'Imagination', in *Sartre*, edited by M. Warnock (Garden City: Anchor, 1971). Reprinted from *British Analytical Philosophy*, edited by B. Williams and A. Montefiore (London: Routledge & Kegan Paul, 1966).

15 Ishiguro, 'Imagination', in Warnock (ed.) *Sartre*, p. 118.

16 One possible class of exceptions is seeing persons, things, facts as they really are. But, even here, when Pierre has shown his stripes and I see him as he really is, for what he really is, I don't say I see Pierre as Pierre.

17 There are also here perhaps the first clues to the problem of the present reference or denotation of the image. We know that among the experiences which can account or allow for my seeing Pierre's face in the doodle is my having met the man Pierre, actually having seen that person, some years ago in Cambridge. But we must also allude to that experience and to other elements in my personal history, as well as to my present context and longings, aversions, adversions and, sometimes, my plans and hopes for the future, to explain an image of Pierre not as he was, then, in Cambridge, but as he is now, in Paris.

18 I have been, I am, diverting attention from the fact that the 'see . . . as . . .' formula cannot be straightforwardly enlisted in a redescription of the particular examples Mead chooses to cite. ('I saw the line of type as correct' strikes me as forced, and 'I saw him as my friend' would seem to me to find its most common service in an exclamation of betrayal, a realization of some acquaintance's insincerity.) The diversion is only temporary, and it is only to follow this line of thought to a natural conclusion. Factors connected with the awkwardness of Mead's examples will be explored then, in the sequel.

19 This is not to confront the question of whether all perception involves interpretation. (For an influential contemporary exposition of an affirmative answer to this question, see E. H. Gombrich's *Art & Illusion: A Study in the Psychology of Pictorial Representation* (Princeton: Princeton University Press, 1960, rev. edn 1961), especially pp. 88,

105, 204–6, 222–8, 297–8, 303, 327–8.) We should also record, given the preceding discussion, that even Sartre, despite his insistence that 'image and . . . perception . . . exclude each other', finds himself saying: 'It is . . . evident that I always *perceive more and otherwise* than I see. . . . [This is] the very structure of perception. . . . The problem [of explaining 'why perception includes *more*'] would be simpler if we would once and for all give up that creature of reason which we know as pure sensation' (*I*, pp. 231–3; *I(e)*, pp. 138–9). It seems to me that, even conceding the idea that ordinary perception is influenced by or is in part a function of attitudes and expectations, we can, within a perimeter marked by that concession, still draw the distinctions between sketched and to be sketched above.

20 P. F. Strawson, 'Imagination and Perception', in L. Foster and J. W. Swanson (eds) *Experience and Theory* (Amherst: University of Massachusetts Press, 1970), p. 31.

CHAPTER 3: THE SELF AS AN OBJECT OF IMAGINATION

1 Descartes, *Second Mediation*, in Elizabeth Anscombe and Peter T. Geach trans. and eds, *Descartes: Philosophical Writings* (London: Nelson, 1969), p. 71.
2 Ibid., p. 70.
3 See, for example, his convoluted footnote on pp. 186–7 of *MSS*. It includes the peculiar claim that '[w]hat may be indicated to others or one's self and does not respond to such gestures of indication is, in the field of perception, what we call a physical thing. The human body is, especially in its analysis, regarded as a physical thing.' If the phrase 'in its analysis' is meant to suggest, say, 'as a collection of carbon, oxygen, nitrogen, (etc.) atoms', to suggest a study of the body as a specimen of organic chemistry, then it would be true, but tautologous, that the human body is regarded as a physical thing. We could also, presumably, analyze ourselves and others in terms which would provoke no responses from us as analysands. And, on the other hand, it is clear that we often find a 'gesture of indication' toward a living 'human body' drawing a response.
4 William James, *Pragmatism* (Cambridge: Harvard University Press, 1978), p. 121.
5 Gilbert Ryle, *The Concept of Mind* (New York: Barnes & Noble, 1949), p. 271.
6 Ibid., p. 257.
7 Ibid., p. 259.
8 Ibid., p. 266.
9 Ibid., p. 264.
10 J. L. Austin, 'Pretending', in J. O. Urmson and G. J. Warnock (eds), *Philosophical Papers* (Oxford: Clarendon Press, 1961), p. 215.
11 Ibid., p. 216.

12 G. E. M. Anscombe, 'Pretending', in S. Hampshire (ed.) *Philosophy of Mind* (New York: Harper & Row, 1966), p. 299. Reprinted from *Proceedings of the Aristotelian Society, Supplementary Volume* (1958), vol. XXXII.
13 Ibid.
14 Jean Piaget, *The Moral Judgment of the Child*, trans. Marjorie Gabain (New York: Free Press, 1965), p. 92.
15 It must be admitted, after all, that an understanding of play in terms of pretending and imagining does not exactly meet Mead's methodological goals either; but we need not assume that the achievement of those goals is the only aim which can control this discussion. And we have, in any case, already remarked (cf. chapter 1, pp. 39–41, and chapter 2, pp. 59–62) on the fact that the proposed theoretical reliance on imagination would not in any way violate the more basic guidelines imposed by the attraction to an evolutionary, naturalistic account.
16 Ryle, *The Concept of Mind*, p. 258.
17 William James, *The Principles of Psychology* (New York: Dover, 1950), vol. one, p. 294.
18 Marcel Proust, *Remembrance of Things Past, Swann's Way*, trans. C. K. Scott Moncrieff (New York: Vintage Books, 1970), p. 15.
19 Proust, *Remembrance of Things Past, Within a Budding Grove*, p. 352.
20 I cannot resist noting that Mead, in trying to describe the 'I' as the mainspring of reflection which cannot be wound back on itself, falls into an acknowledgment that the mechanism of reflection is imagination. (Cf., e.g., *MSS*, p. 174, fn. 11, and the reference to the 'imaginative presentation of the organism'.)
21 This is not to beg metaphysical questions about reflection and phases of the self. They of course remain for any account, but they lie beyond the issue here.
22 G. H. Mead, *The Philosophy of the Act*, ed. Charles W. Morris, (Chicago: University of Chicago Press, 1938), p. 12.
   Hereafter, references to this work will be made by parenthetical notations, using the abbreviation '*PA*'.
23 James, *The Principles of Psychology*, vol. one, p. 114.
24 John Dewey, *Human Nature and Conduct* (New York: Modern Library, 1922, 1930), p. 66.
25 Cf., for example, *MSS*, pp. 354–78, and Dewey's *Human Nature and Conduct*, pp. 178–86. The idea of this connection between thought, inquiry, and the reorganization of habit is in fact a fundamental pragmatic doctrine. An early version of it appears in C. S. Peirce's 'The Fixation of Belief', originally published in *Popular Science Monthly*, vol. 12 (November 1877), pp. 1–15, available in his *Collected Papers, Vol. V*, ed. Hartshorne and Weiss (Cambridge, Massachusetts: Belknap Press of Harvard, 1934), pp. 223–47.

CHAPTER 4: PROBLEMS OF THE SELF

1 It is clear that self-deception is here thought of as deception not merely by, but also about the self (or its aspects). I would want to defend the idea that cases which could be described in this way do in fact occupy the central territory in need of survey.

Examples which might not seem to fit this description are, of course, presented in the literature. But, for example, the mother who refuses to believe that her son is the murderer, despite her acquaintance with the apparently overwhelming and irrefutable evidence against him, might not be best seen as self-deceived. She might be better explained by, say, an account of what it is to have *faith* in a person. And the scientist who ignores clearly available data which tend to disconfirm her pet theory might be best explained by, for example, an account of *wishful thinking*. The man who seems to the world to be concealing from himself what the world says is plain – that his wife is unfaithful – may simply be, for example, radically inattentive. Or, if the tale is told with more or other details, we might again say that the man has faith in his wife. Or, yet again, he, too, may be in the grip of wishful thinking. Or, to allude to a version of this story which *would* be susceptible to the terms of the account here being developed, he may not see himself as a cuckold.

I certainly cannot insist that every example which might be brought forward to illustrate self-deception will either be explained by the account I am here presenting or be better understood as an instance of some other human capacity or failure. I can only insist 1) that we remember that people may be variously opaque or incoherent and 2) that the cases which *are* caught by this account are at the focus of our attention when we study the puzzle of self-deception.

2 For a summary and discussion of some of the empirical data and literature related to this point, see Morris Rosenberg, *Conceiving the Self* (New York: Basic Books, 1979).
3 Stanley Cavell, *The Claim of Reason*, (New York: Oxford University Press, 1979), p. 369.
4 Jean-Paul Sartre, *Being and Nothingness*, trans. Hazel E. Barnes (New York: Philosophical Library, 1956), p. 59.
5 Sartre, *Being and Nothingness*, p. 55.
6 Herbert Fingarette, *Self-Deception* (London: Routledge & Kegan Paul, 1969), pp. 95–6.
7 Ibid., p. 98.
8 William James, *The Principles of Psychology* (New York: Dover, 1950), vol. II, p. 336.
9 This might be one description of what it would be to have one's body subject to an alien will. (Cf. Cavell, *The Claim of Reason*, p. 383.) The source of this woman's apparent willfulness is her recognition of the object she is in the sight of the other, and, if she is trying to escape it,

then, still, her actions are ultimately directed and powered by that other's glance.
10 Cavell, *The Claim of Reason*, p. 385.
11 And I suppose that in reacting to these interpretations, one generates – or follows one's destiny to – the rest of the relations. For example: the man sees himself as untrustworthy and is disgusted with himself.
12 Cf., again, Wittgenstein's remark that 'Seeing as . . . is like seeing and again not like' (*PI*, II, p. 197) and his claim that 'Seeing an aspect and imagining are subject to the will' (*PI*, II, p. 213).
13 William Hazlitt, *Complete Works*, edited by P. P. Howe (London: J. M. Dent & Sons, Ltd., 1930–1934), vol. VII, p. 385.
    Hereafter, references to this work will be made by parenthetical notations, using the abbreviation '*CW*'.
14 His account of personal identity is similar to – that is, it anticipates – the view recently espoused by Derek Parfit. (Cf. 'Personal Identity', *Philosophical Review*, LXXX. I (January 1971).) Parfit's own view is developed from a Humean basis; and the implications of his version of this account are further explored, along with other matters, in Parfit's *Reasons and Persons* (New York: Oxford University Press, 1984).
15 Parfit, *Reasons and Persons*, p. 308.

INDEX

absence, imagery and, 44, 54, 59, 62
accessibility, habits' lack of, 99–100; of psychological datum, 5–6
action, habits of, 126; role in seeing as, 61; self-interested, 129; spontaneity of, 91–2; voluntary, 127–9
actors and acting, 32–3, 36–7, 49–50, 73, 79, 80, 81; *see* performances; pretending; roles, taking of
affect, as motivating, 92, 125; *see* cognitive/affective distinction
alien will, subjection to, 143n9
altruism, 131; *see* benevolence
Anscombe, G. E. M., 81
apprehension of oneself, as a whole, 73; *see* imaginative apprehension
attitudes, as beginnings of acts, 43; as constituting character, 87–8; expression of, 80, 114; functional interpretation of, 137n1; as involved in perception, 141; as objects of interpretation, 114; organization of (as generalized other), 24, 77, 85–6; of others, 25, 35, 77–8, 125–6; self-interested, 131; self as structure of, 88; words (or symbols) and, 28, 34
attributions (or, ascriptions), first-person, 67–9, 105; of self-deception, 12, 110–12
Austin, J. L., 58, 80–1

authentic self, 104
authenticity, in social interchange, 37, 87, 90
autonomy, 11; generalized other and, 86–9, 95

bad faith, 104, 105, 110, 115–17; *see* self-deception
Baldwin, J. M., 82
behavior, as conduct, 135n2; deliberate, 19; potential, 70; public, 69–70; *see* reponse(s)
behaviorism, 60, 74; Mead and, 5, 34, 44; Watson and, 2; *see* functional explanation; social behaviorism
behaviorist account of imagination, 10, 42, 78; – of meaning, 30–2, 34
believing, apparent, 67–9
benevolence, disinterested, 126
Berger, Peter, 4
Bergson, Henri, 9
Bernstein, Basil, 8
biologic individual, 'I' as, 93; self vs., 67; *see* body
biological basis (of self), 11, 15, 17, 27, 83
body, as corpse, 72; as instrument of expression, 33; self and, 10, 27, 66–72, 141n3

Index

caricature, 48–9, 54
Cavell, Stanley, 113–14; on ignorance of the self, 124
character, as attitudes, 87–8; child's lack of, 100
chimera, image of, 56, 57, 140n12
cognitive/affective distinction, 36, 37
coherent self, 84, 88
common perspective, 106–7
community, language as basis of, 7; sense of, 103; (or, social) validation, 123; voice of, 90–1
community's perspective (or, interpretation), 106–7, 110, 111–12, 114, 117, 121; on being the object of, 115–16; self-knowledge and, 122
complete self, 24, 78, 85
conceptions of world, 71
conduct, behavior as, 135n2; of community, 107, 110; *see* individual conduct; social conduct
conformity, autonomy and, 86–9
conscious communication, distinguished by responses to meaning, 34; emotion and, 36–7; as involving shared responses, 31, 34
consciousness, 2, 5; habits and, 100–1; images in, 44; selective nature of, 62; social activity and, 14
consentient set (of perspectives), 106–7
contact, non-perspectival sense of, 76; ultimate experience of, 98
control (of activity), 19, 23; *see* self-control; social control
conversation, 37, fashioning oneself in, 87; of gestures, 17–20; inner, 42
Cooley, Charles Horton, 39–41
corporeal (substance), 2; self and, 10, 66–72
creativity, 93

Darwin, Charles, Darwinian theory, 7; *see* evolutionary theory
deliberation, pretending and, 80–1; as reorganization of habit, 101, 142n25
Descartes, 1–3, 6, 49, 66–7, 69, 109, 138n6
Dewey, John, 4, 5; on habit, 101–2

discord, *see* harmony
dualism, mind-body, 3, 42, 66–7
duck-rabbit, 59, 63, 113–14

egocentricity, 6, 11–13; alleged metaphysical priority of, 12, 125–33; *see* selfishness
empathy, 130
empiricist (and rationalist) accounts of person, 6; – of imagination, 9, 45, 62
epistemology, 120; and metaphysics, 95; *see* vision; knowledge
essential poverty (of images), 51
evolutionary theory, 7; language and, 21; self-concern and, 130–1; *see* phylogeny
expression, readiness for, 80, 83
external world, distinguishing self from, 82

fact, of the matter, 115, 118–19, 122–3; imagination as natural –, 40–1; self-concern as natural –, 131
fact/value distinction, 120
fancying, 78; *see* imagining
field of congruence, among perspectives, 96
figure/ground picture, 63
Fingarette, Herbert, 118–19
freedom, personal, 11; sense of, 91; social control and, 89–91
Freud, Sigmund, 82
functional explanation (of mind), 137n1
future, of others, 127; personal connection to, 12, 127–8; reference of imagery to, 46; self, 127

games, 10; as stage toward self-consciousness, 23–6
Gassendi, Pierre, 138n6
generalized other, 23–4, 26, 77; as abstracted common attitudes, 95; autonomy and, 86–90; as organization of attitudes, 85–6; scientific perspective and, 95–9, 106
gestures, conversation of, 17–20; shared responses and, 78
ghosts and 'doubles', 71

Index

Gombrich, E. H., 140n19
good (and evil), 128; child's pursuit of, 131–2

habits, deliberation as reorganisation of, 101, 142n25; as distinct from self, 93–4; function(s) of, 11, 100; 'I' and, 93–4; routine vs. intelligent, 101; self and, 99–102
hallucinations and dreams, 52, 139n10, 139n11
harmony, among interpretations of self, 120; lack of in self-deception, 111; between people in society, 89; of perspectives, 99; of responses, 21; search for, 132–3; social, 103; unstable, 117, 119
Harré, Rom, 7
having a self, as bound with knowing that self, 124, 125
Hazlitt, William, 12; on natural interest in others, 126–9, 131–2
herding, phenomenon of, 17–18
Hume, David, 51, 62, 144n14

'I', 66–7; habits and, 93–4; as mainspring of reflection, 142n20; as spontaneity, subjectivity, distinct from 'me', 91–3
ideas, as faint perceptions, 51, 138n5, 138–9n9; as objects of imagination, 128
identification, imaginative, 39, 84–5; with others' perceptions, 74–5
illusions, deceived by, 139n11; visual, 58
Images (and imagery), 42–57, 60, 138n6; as adjustments of organism, 46; corporeal, 66–7; deliberately produced, 52, 139n9; Hume on, 51; and the image family, 54; representational material of, 54; as response provoking, 43; as sui generis consciousness, 47; *see* mental image(s)
imaginary, 1; objects, 55, 60; playmate, 22–3
imagination, 1, 2; as cognitive and affective, 125; as contemplating a corporeal likeness, 67; Cooley on, 41; faculty of, 178; family of concepts of, 64; foresight through, 128; as foundation for interested action, 129; habits and, 102; as link to others, 125; Mead on, 42–6; as mechanism of reflection, 142n20; objects of, 44, 128; Sartre on, 46–57, 138–9n9, 139n11, 140–1n19; Sartre vs. Mead, 57–62; self-reflective act of, 108, 125; social dimension of, 13, 102; traditional account of, 45; *see* perception (imagination and)
imaginative absorption, 84
imaginative apprehension (or, grasp), 13, 49, 63, 102; of self, 92, 93, 108, 125
imaginative capacity, 39
imaginative consciousness, 54–6; object of, 55–6
imaginative projection, 139n9
imaginative rehearsal, 102
imagining, as attending to images, 55; as exercise of mental faculty, 1; as functionless, 2; of objects, 50; and perceiving, 47–8, 51–2, 57–9; and pretending, 78–81, 83–5; 'seeing as' and, 61; *see* visualizing
imitation, 22, 54, 80
impersonation, 49, 54, 81
impressions, Humean, 51
impulse, 102
impulsive responses, 101
individual and society, conflict between, 90
individual conduct, self-deception and, 111
individual perspective, 106, 107, 110, 114
individualistic social psychology, *see* Cooley
ink-blot, Rorschach, *see* interpretation, standard
inquiry, social character of, 3
intelligent action, habits and, 100
intention(ality), general theory of, 119; play and, 82; pretending and, 81–2;

Index

visual representations and, 54; *see* mental images (material and meaning of)
interaction(s), social, 90; directed toward satisfaction, 120
interest, in past or present, 126; in future, 126; object of, 128; visualizing and, 62
interpretation(s), imaginative act of, 10; individual's vs. community's, 115; mutually satisfying, 120–1; one obscured by another, 113–14; and perspective, 108; standard, 110, 114; *see* self-interpretation
interpretative contexts, 'seeing as' and, 60, 62–5
intersection of perspectives, scientist's depiction of, 96–7
introspection, 3, 15, 16, 122
Ishiguro, Hide, 55–6, 58

James, William, 4, 9; on conceptions of world, 71, 136n6; on habit, 100; on social selves, 86–7; on truth, 120

knowledge, as co-ordination of perspectives, 96; as intersection of perspectives, 96, 106; theory of, 108

language, emergence of, 21; gestures and, 18; reflexivity and, 39; shared meaning and, 20, 30–2; socialization and, 7–8
logical type (or, category), 80

maturation, as complete self-development, 85–6, 88, 95; and habits, 99–100; *see* personality
'me', as social object, 91–2
Mead, George Herbert: on coordination of perspectives, 105–8, 115; on imagination, 42–8, 50, 57–65; introductory remarks on, 4–11; on nature and development of self, 14–41; and proposed alternative account of self, 66–103 (passim); *see* generalized other; reflexivity; roles; social process; vocal gesture

meaning, 18, 20, 30–2, 34; *see* response
mechanisms of mind, 126, 129
memory, 15, 66, 126, 129
mental (phenomena), 1, 5; *see* psychical entities
mental image(s), as constituents of perceptual world, 43–4; material and meaning of, 54, 56–7, 138n6; neurological account of, 61; postulation of, 60; relational analysis of, 55; *see* images (and imagery)
mention selection, 140n12
metaphysics, 40, 41, 42; and epistemology, 95; *see* selfishness (the metaphysical hypothesis of)
methodologies, of inquiry, 3, 6, 9–10, 40, 82
mind, 1, 5; Cartesian, 14, 66; distinctively human, 7; *see* self (as mind)
mirrors, 32–3
mock-actions, 78
modern man (and social order), 90
moral agent, 126
moral instruction (and/or training), 126
moral problem, self deception as, 103; failure to sympathize as, 130
Morris, Charles W., 95–6, 106

native capacities, 39–41
nothingness, *see* absence
novelty, of future, 46; 'I' as source of, 91–3
null extensions, terms with, 140n12

objective reference (of images), 44–6, 140n17
objective world, images in, 42–6; *see* perception (imagination and); worlds
objectivity, Mead's account of, 106–8; in describing bad faith, 118; of 'I' and 'me', 92; pragmatic account of, 115; of self-apprehension, 28, 69–70
ontogeny, of self-consciousness, 7, 22–7; of (apparent) selfishness, 131–2
original self, 87

Index

otherness, 35, 36, 38, 132; *see* generalized other

Parfit, Derek, 130–1, 144n14
Pegasus, image of, 45
Peirce, Charles Sanders, 4, 142n25
perception, imagination and, 46–57, 138n6, 138n9, 139n11; as involving interpretation, 63, 140n19; *see* quasi-observation; 'seeing as'
perceptual world, 43; *see* objective world
performances, personal, 81; sophisticated (rehearsed) and naive, 80, 81
Perky, C. W. (Perky effect), 138–9n9
personal identity, criteria of, 3; Hazlitt on, 127; Parfit on, 144n14
personality, maturity of, 85–6, 88, 95, 99–100; ontogenesis of, 25; social, 87, 91
perspective(s), convergence of, 122, 125; coordination of, 96; imagination and, 76; importance to self-development, 86; individual vs. community, 106–8, 110, 114; organization of, 115; of others, 35; senses and, 75–6; *see* community's perspective
Peters, R. S., 8
phenomenological description, conjecture vs., 57
philosophy, Mead and the discipline of, 4, 5, 7, 9; on puzzle of socialization, 8; on self, 10, 12; *see* epistemology; metaphysics
photograph, 48–50, 54, 61
phylogenesis of self, 7, 17–22
physiological organism; *see* body
Piaget, Jean, 82
plane of events, 96–7
plasticity, 93
play, 10; on concept of, 83; as stage of self-development, 22–3, 26, 78–85
play and games, 74, 77–89; as emblematic of self-developmental processes, 24; fundamental difference between, 85; unified self and, 99–100

portraits, 48–9, 52–4
pragmatism, American movement of, 4, 120; as anti-Cartesian, 3; evolutionary theory and, 7, 21; Mead's, 10, 74, 108
present and past, interest in, 126; objects of self-interested action, 129
pretending, 78–81, 83–5; understanding play in terms of, 142n15
principles (person's), as community attitudes, 88
private phenomena, 1, 3, 6; images as, 44, 60; *see* mental; subjectivity
Proust, Marcel, on multiple selves, on authenticity, 87
psychical entities, 137n1; images as, 1, 42–5; meanings as, 30
psychology, scientific, 99; social, 4
public phenomena, 3, 10, 60–1, 69; *see* objective world
pure sensation, 140–1n19

quasi-observation, of imagery, 50–3

rationality, reflexivity and, 15–16; shared responses and, 37
reality; *see* conceptions of world
reflection, imaginative act of, 10, 11; metaphysical questions about, 142n21; words, deeds and, 68–9, 85; *see* self-reflection
reflexiveness, 8
reflexivity, of body, 72; essence of self, 7, 9, 10, 14, 67; imagination as core of, 78; play and, 23; total, 26, 72–6; vocal gesture and, 26–8
regulated procedures, games marked by, 87
res cogitans, 2; *see* self as mind
response(s), awareness of own, 19–20; imagination and (shared), 102; implicit, 31–2; sharing of, 20, 25, 30, 34–6
responsibility, 103
role(s), organization of in play, 22–3, 77; 'seeing as' and, 69; social, 8, 73, 93, 116; as socially-defined, 116, 117;

sustaining of, 116, 124–5; taking of, 24, 25, 78–81, 83, 90; whimsical adoption of, 95
Rosenberg, Morris, 143n2
rule (or, vote), majority, 107, 110
rules, 23; games marked by, 87
Ryle, Gilbert, 1, 49, 78, 80–1, 84, 138n6

Sapir, Edward, 7
Sartre, Jean-Paul, 9; on bad faith, 115–21; on imagination, 46–57
Scheffler, Israel, 136n4, 137n1, 140n12
secret inner core (of self), 70
'seeing as', 10, 53, 58–65, 73–5, 110; forced redescriptions in terms of, 140n18; seeing oneself as, 69–71, 108, 112–13, 124–5; 'seeing things as they really are', 140n16
self, biological basis of, 11, 15; as emergent, 14; etymology of word, 15–16; as given, 6; ignorance of, 124; language and, 7–8; as mind, 1–3; as mosaic, 108–9, 113; multiplicity of, 86–7, 127; as object of imagination, 9, 10, 66–103, 112; reflexivity of, 9, 15, 16, 95, 100; as structure of attitudes, 88, 132; unity and unification of, 10, 11, 24, 73, 74, 76, 85, 88, 95, 99, 103; *see* body (self and); Mead
self-acquaintance, 66
self-alienation, 29
self-audition, 136n6; *see* words, relation to
self-awareness, 32; habits and, 100; play and, 84; sporadic character of, 111; *see* self-consciousness
self-centeredness, 130, 131; *see* egocentricity
self-concern, 131; *see* self-interest
self-consciousness, intuitive, 3; ontogenesis of, 22–7, 77; problem of, 16; in conduct, 15, 87
self-control, self-awareness and, 32–4, 86
self-deceiver, as hiding truth, 113; perversity of, 112
self-deception, 11, 12, 103; as deception about self, 143n1; conflict of, 116; and misconstrual of others, 132; inconsistency and, 109, 111; locus of incoherency, 110; puzzle of, 105, 109, 111; social self and, 103–22; ubiquity of, 104–5; willfulness of, 109, 112, 113
self-description, 70
self-image, 112, 125
self-interest, 11–13, 125–33; as acquired, 128
self-interpretation, 73, 110–13, 121, 144n11; activity and passivity of, 124–5; and the past, 129
self-knowledge, 11–12, as activity, 124; as convergence of perspectives, 122–5; and social validation, 122–4, 125
self-love, 126; non-innateness of, 131; as originally impersonal, 128
self-objectification, 69–70, 82
self-possession, 85, 131
self-reflection, as requisite for self-deception, 111
selfishness, the metaphysical hypothesis of, 127, 129; as natural human trait, 126, 130–1
sensuous contents of experience, images as, 44–5
separateness, 129, 132
sight, objects of, 71, 76; *see* vision
significant symbol(s), 8, 18, 31, 34
sketch, 48–9, 61, 138n6
social accommodation (or, adjustment), 32, 33, 86
social act(ivity), of animals, 17; common, 78; consciousness and, 14; cooperative, 24; human, 19; language and, 21; meaning and, 30
social behaviorism, 6, 7, 9, 10, 15
social conduct, self arises in, 26–7; *see* conduct of community
social context (or, setting), 3, 6, 24; as factor in interpretation, 59–60; and self-concern, 131
social control, 11; freedom and, 89–91; self-governance and, 32
social genesis, of self, 6; *see* Mead, on

Index

nature and development of self
social interaction, 10, 19, 24, 36–8, 102–3, 125; verbal, 38
socialization, 7–8
social object(s), 89–90; self as, 94
social organization, 89–91; vocal gesture as medium of, 21; whole, 24
social process(es), 10, 24; as biological precondition of self, 15, 77; constituting objects via language (symbols), 38, 136–7n6; *see* conceptions of world
social sciences, 7, 8, 9; *see* psychology; sociology
social self, 13, 86–9; imagination and, 39–41, 102–3; *see* Mead, on nature and development of self
social-deception, 116
societal development, 14, 89–90, 101
society, animal, 14, 40, 97, 131; as function of mind, 40
sociology, 4, 40
soul, *see* mind
speech, 8, 28, 36, 136n6; *see* vocal gesture
standard interpretation, 110, 114; *see* community (or, social) validation; interpretation(s)
stimulation, reciprocal, 17–18; self-, 20, 21
Strawson, P. F., 64
Stryker, Sheldon, 4
subjectivity, 6, 40; 'I' as, 91; of other, 13, 125
symbolic interactionism, 4
symbolic systems, 8
symbols, noises as, 8; power of, 38, 136–7n6
symmetry, of responses, 20, 28; of speaker and listener, 32
sympathetic identification, doctrine of, 129
sympathetic imagination, 12, 129–30, 132
sympathetic link, 13, 125
sympathy, 12–13, 121, 130, 131; self-, 37; true, 132
synthetic whole, 97

theory of knowledge, germ of, 108; *see* epistemology
'treating as', 61; bodies (as) corpses, 72; *see* 'seeing as'
Trilling, Lionel, 13
truth, hiding of, 113; about persons, 115, 119–20; pragmatic theory of, 12, 120; *see* fact
type (of an object), science's concern with, 98; seen from perspective of generalized other, 99

ultimate perspective (of physical science), 97–8
unity of self, 10, 85–9, 94, 99–100
unreal objects, 139n11; *see* chimera; Pegasus
unselfish acts, 126
utopias, 103
utterances, 10, 27, 31, 34, 36, 73; *see* vocal gesture

vision, epistemological preeminence of, 75
visualizing, 47, 50–1, 61–3, 54, 75, 78, 79; *see* imagining
vocal gesture, 7, 8, 10, 20–2, 25, 66, 78; reflexivity and, 27–32, 39, 72–4
voice, of reason, of past, 90; of future, of community, 91; *see* speech; words, relation to
von Humbolt, Wilhelm, 7

Watson, James B., 2, 42–3
welfare of others, 126–7
Whitehead, Alfred North, 5
whole of self, 27, 72–4, 85, 103, 108–9, 111–13
Whorf, Benjamin, 7
will; *see* voluntary action
Williams, Bernard, 54–6
Wittgenstein, Ludwig, 10; on being struck by a likeness, 61; on the flashing of an aspect, 57; on imagining as subject to will, 144n12; on 'objects' of sight, 70–1; on relation to one's words, 28; on 'seeing as', 58–9, 67–8, 144n12; on

understanding others, 37–8; *see* duck-rabbit

words, creative power of, 38; relation to, 28–30, 32, 136n6; *see* reflection; speech; vocal gesture

worlds, phenomenal and physical, 44; real and imaginary, 56, 61; *see* objective world

Wundt, Wilhelm, definition of gesture, 18–19